SPAIN

THE HORIZON CONCISE HISTORY OF

SPAIN

by Melveena McKendrick

Published by
AMERICAN HERITAGE PUBLISHING CO., INC.
New York

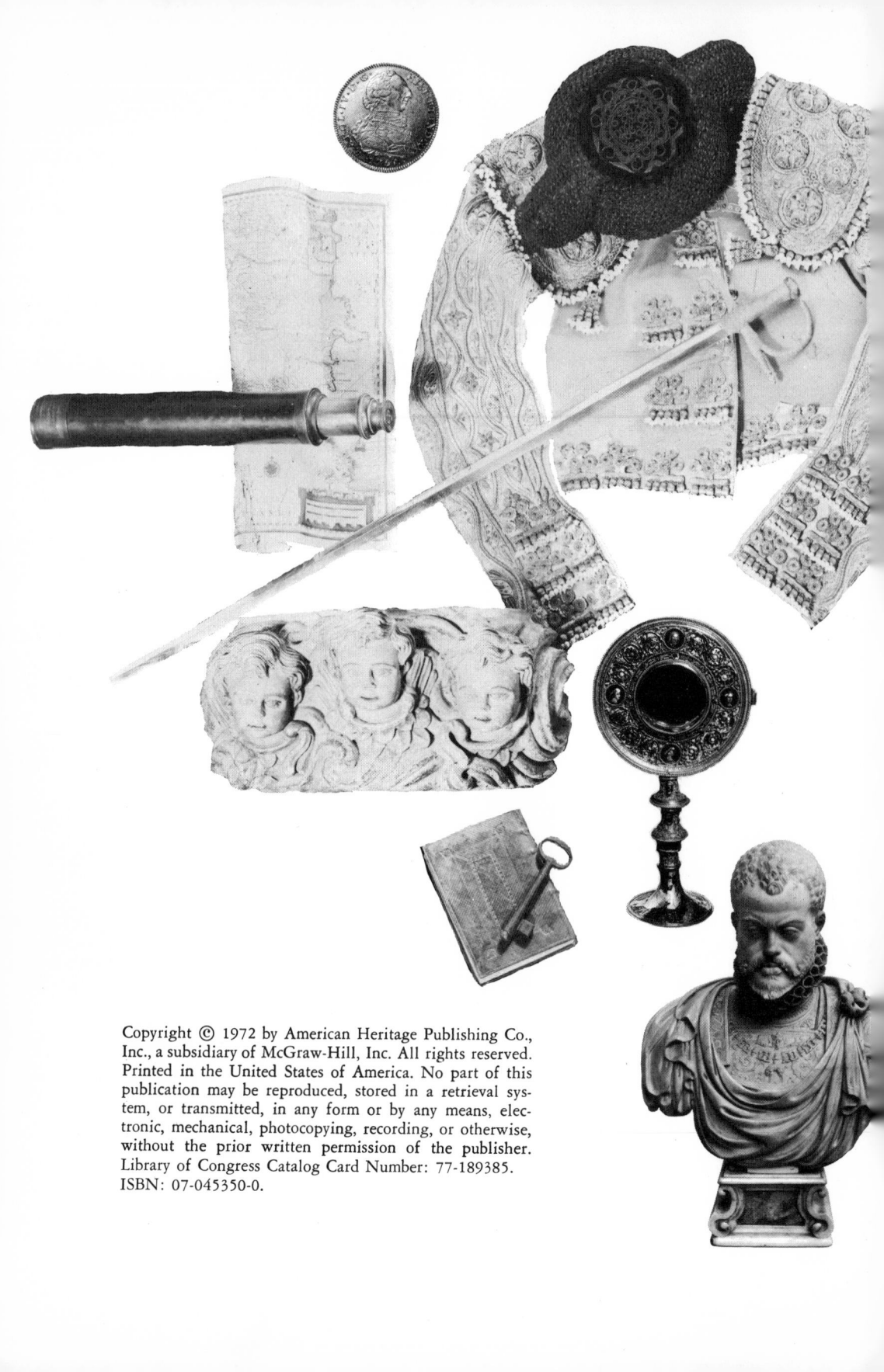

FOREWORD

The history of Spain is an enigma about which historians have not even begun to agree. Out of the division and strife of the Middle Ages she emerged from behind the massive barrier of the Pyrenees to straddle the stage of European politics like some new colossus. She discovered a New World, became the greatest power on earth, and created a Golden Age of culture quite breathtaking in the quality of its achievement. Within a hundred and fifty years she was in an advanced state of decay and fast being left behind by a more progressive, capitalism-oriented Europe. Since then the story of Spain has been in the main a story of political, economic, and educational backwardness that culminated in modern times in the ultimate tragedy of full-blown civil war. Spain herself has not remained oblivious to this bitter anomaly. Her writers and thinkers have seared their souls in efforts to find the key. But no answer has seemed to be adequate.

Nevertheless, there are certain basic facts relevant to the history of Spain, whose potential influence on her fate cannot be ignored with impunity. Geographically, Spain was by European standards seriously underendowed at birth. After Switzerland it is at once the most mountainous and the highest country in Europe, while in the impoverished aridness of its terrain it is second to none. Although Spain is predominantly an agricultural country, a mere 10 per cent of its soil can be called rich, whereas 45 per cent is more or less totally unproductive. The great central tableland with its bastions of mountain ranges makes it a country difficult to cross, a situation aggravated by the fact that only two of its rivers—the Ebro and the Guadalquivir—are of any use in agriculture and navigation. Over this forbidding surface rages a climate of fierce extremes. Galicia enjoys constant rainfall,while on the southeast coast rain is an occasion for wild rejoicing. On the central *meseta* the Castilians have to withstand bitter cold and freezing winds in winter and torrid heat and drought in summer—"nine months of winter and three of hell," as they expressively put it.

The divided nature of the land has encouraged and perpetuated a social and linguistic fragmentation. The country is in effect a collection of states or kingdoms—Galicia, the Basque Provinces, Aragon, Navarre, Catalonia, Valencia, León, Murcia, Extremadura, Asturias, Castile, and Andalusia—each of which has a strong consciousness of its individuality and only the last three of which naturally speak Castilian. Although Castile eventually succeeded in imposing unification on these states, Aragon tried to secede from the union as late as the seventeenth century, while the Basques and the Catalans are determined separatists even today. Entrenched regionalism and a much less than bountiful nature might seem to promise trouble enough. But to these has to be added the fact—which makes Spain unique in Europe—of nearly eight hundred years of occupation by, and enforced coexistence with, an alien religion and culture with which it refused to integrate: Islam.

No doubt much more of Spanish history is explicable in terms of the course of European history as a whole than was hitherto thought. But the complex amalgam of civilizations and races that is Spain does have its distinctive problems and does seem to live more in the shadow of its past than most countries. The limits of speculation will doubtless be pushed further and further back as systematic research into the crevices of Spanish history continues, but the richness of the weave of Spain's history will always admit of speculation, and herein lies its fascination. From the story that follows, the reader will certainly draw his own conclusions.

CHAPTER I

EARLY SPAIN

Spain's geographical position has rendered her a natural focus for the attentions of a varied succession of migrants, traders, colonizers, and conquerors. Thrusting massively out of the southwestern corner of Europe and separated from the continent of Africa by a bare eight miles of readily crossed sea, she closes off the Mediterranean from the Atlantic and faces Asia across the inland sea whose shores saw the dawn of our civilization. From the north, from the south, and from the east came prehistoric tribes, Celts, Phoenicians, Greeks, Carthaginians, Romans, Barbarians, Arabs, and Africans, in obedience to their respective needs and compulsions, in search of *lebensraum,* empire, converts, booty, or trade.

About the earliest inhabitants of the Peninsula little is known with certainty. Upper Paleolithic man, whose origins are vague, bequeathed us some record of his hunter's life in the wall paintings in the caves of Altamira and Castillo. Neolithic man has rewarded archaeological research with artifacts of a different culture, pointing to agriculture and animal husbandry, rudimentary houses and metalworking. Toward the beginning of the second millennium B.C., a wave of megalith wor-

A paleolithic cave painting from Castellón shows a bowman hunting deer.

shipers from the East initiated a period of agrarian prosperity and skilled craftsmanship in Andalusia in the south, while in the north another megalithic people settled in the Pyrenees to become the ancient precursors of the Basques, a race with a language whose roots still remain a mystery to philologists.

With the introduction of bronze metallurgy between 1900 and 1600 B.C. by a people who settled in Almería, Andalusia reached its peak of early civilization and entered the realm of legend as a land of fabulous riches and prosperity. Its capital was Tartessus—known in the Bible as Tarshish and conjecturally situated in the Guadalquivir Valley—and it was the silver of Tartessus that drew the eyes of the trading east and brought the Phoenicians to Spain. A short distance along the coast they founded the city of Gadir, the modern Cádiz, before 800 B.C. In time the Phoenicians established trading settlements along the south and east coasts of the Peninsula and in the Balearics. Although they were uninterested in colonization, their superior commercial and technical knowledge, and their cultural contacts, carved a deep impression upon the civilization of their adopted country. The Phoenicians also disclosed Spain to the civilized world, and with them the Peninsula emerged from its prehistoric penumbra and set foot upon the stage of Mediterranean history.

In the sixth century B.C. the example set by the Phoenicians was followed by their trading rivals the Greeks, lured westward by tales of the silver of Cartagena, the gold of the Sierra Morena, and the copper of Río Tinto. Their settlement at Emporion (Spanish Ampurias) in Catalonia succeeded Massilia (Marseilles) as Greece's principal port of trade in the western Mediterranean. Like the Phoenicians, the Greeks settled and traded along the southern and eastern coasts, adding another layer of civilization to these already comparatively cosmopolitan areas and bringing wealth to the inhabitants. Their superior culture enriched native art and, more practically, they introduced into the Peninsula two plants, the olive tree and the grapevine, which have played a crucial part in Spain's agriculture ever since.

By the time the Greeks reached Spain, the peoples living there on the east coast had come to be known as Iberians—a term now taken not as indicating a specific race of people, but as a generic label for the complex group of inhabitants of the Peninsula's Mediterranean coast from Catalonia to Andalusia. Little is known about these Iberians. What is clear is that they were quite distinct from the people of the interior. For while the Phoenicians and the Greeks were busy developing trade in the east, the interior was witnessing equally important events of a different order. Between 900 and 600 B.C. successive waves of Celts on their migrations through Europe from Asia penetrated the Pyrenees and, spreading over the central *meseta,* occupied much of Spain. All warrior peoples of Indo-European stock in search of new homes, they settled with ease amongst the natives of the north and west, and opened up hitherto unpopulated land in the center.

Naturally, Celts and Iberians did not remain entirely separate. On the great central plateau they mingled and interbred to form the hard core of the Peninsula's native substratum, the Celtiberians. Traditionally the Celts were regarded as a race of violent, rustic shepherds and the Iberians as pacific farmers and urban dwellers, but the reality, it is now felt, must have been more complex. The Celts have a clearer identity than the Iberians and we know that they brought to Spain the broad sword, the technique of iron metallurgy, and trousers. But even so, our knowledge of their way of life is severely limited because they also brought their custom of the ritual burning of the dead. And the dead are normally a major source of archaeological information.

After Nebuchadnezzar besieged Tyre in 586–573 B.C. and North African Carthage succeeded to Phoenicia's commercial empire, mineral attractions of the Iberian Peninsula once more exerted influence. Before long, Carthage was able to claim the western Mediterranean for her own, and although the Greeks continued to trade in sporadic fashion along the east coast of Spain, Carthage soon acquired a commercial hegemony in southern Spain which she managed to retain for the next two to three hundred years. Greek artifacts—bronze statues in the Sierra Morena and Corinthian helmets near Huelva—give way to evidence of Carthaginian sculpture, jewelry, and ceramics, while to the agricultural skills introduced by their predecessors the new traders added their expertise in fish curing and in the production of esparto grass. While the Carthaginians thus added to the ever deepening civilization of the south and east, their most significant bequest to Spain was on an order of magnitude out of all proportion to their direct influence. For they were responsible for bringing the Romans to the land

in the far west, and making it the scene of Rome's greatest military struggle, the Second Punic War.

The First Punic War, in which Rome and Carthage had contested for Sicily, had ended indecisively in 241 B.C., but it had allowed the natives of the Iberian Peninsula to regain control of their land. However, the need for treasure and the strategic potential of Spain had led the Carthaginians under Hamilcar Barca to set about reasserting and extending Carthage's influence in the Peninsula. And what had formerly been commercial rule began to take on the suspicious look of an attempt at empire. When a Carthaginian capital was established at Carthago Nova (modern Cartagena) on the east coast, Rome decided that some limit ought to be imposed upon the Carthaginian Empire in Spain. Her envoys consequently elicited from Carthage a pledge not to advance northward beyond the Ebro River.

The situation was an explosive one and explode it inevitably did. The immediate cause of the explosion was the Iberian town of Sagun-

Celtic warriors, armed with helmets, swords, and shields such as those above, invaded Spain from the north bringing a distinctive language and culture.

tum which lay a hundred or so miles south of the Ebro but enjoyed
Roman protection—an ideal departure point for a Roman take-over
bid. Rome therefore intervened in Saguntum's affairs to promote interests hostile to Carthage. The outcome of this double dealing was that
in 219 Hannibal, Hamilcar's young son, who had been Carthaginian
commander in Spain since 221, laid siege to Saguntum. Eight months
later, after a long and bitter struggle, the city fell. Hannibal had broken
no treaty: Saguntum was well within Carthaginian territory and was
not among those allies of Rome which Carthage had pledged itself not
to attack. Nevertheless Roman prestige was seen to be at issue. An
ultimatum was given in the form of a demand for the surrender of
Hannibal. It was refused and the two powers were at war. The struggle for Spain and for hegemony in the Mediterranean had begun.

Both sides simultaneously decided to carry the war straight to the
nub of the opposition. In 218, as Hannibal and his elephants made their
famous trek over the Alps to Italy, two Roman legions with sea support
landed at Emporion in Spain. A few miles from Tarragona, the legions
met and routed a force of 11,000 Carthaginians, and within two
months the country north of the Ebro was securely in Roman hands.
The following years, however, did not bring such easy successes for
Rome, although the natives helped by snapping constantly at the
Carthaginians' heels. Hannibal's brother, Hasdrubal, and Publius
Scipio and his brother, Cornelius, snarled and attacked like rival
wolves, without gaining much significant headway. The turning point
came in 218 at the Battle of Dertosa on the north bank of the Ebro.
The defeat suffered by the Carthaginians at the hands of the two
Scipios was the first real threat to their empire in the Iberian Peninsula.
Not until 210, however, as Hannibal's fortunes in Italy declined, was
it possible for reinforcements to be sent to northern Spain to strengthen
the Roman position. In the meantime the formidable Scipio had been
killed and Rome's native recruits had deserted. A year later Carthago
Nova itself fell before the daring onslaught of Scipio Africanus, son of
the dead Publius, and the legions he had molded into a redoubtable
army forced their way into southern Spain and the Guadalquivir Valley. In 206 Carthage's first, foremost, and last colony in Spain, Cádiz,
made terms with Scipio Africanus. Roman rule in Spain had begun.

Carthage, however, was not all Rome had to contend with in Spain, as she soon learned. One of the earliest provinces to be acquired by the Romans under the Republic, the Iberian Peninsula was also one of the last to be truly pacified. The mountainous nature of the terrain and the fierce independence of the native tribes, particularly in the north, center, and west, made conquest a difficult and piecemeal affair: it took the legions of Rome the staggering period of two hundred years to bring the country to heel. One frustrated general after another discovered Spain to be the natural home of guerrilla warfare.

With the acquisition of Carthaginian Spain in 206 B.C., the Romans immediately set about the organization of the new province. The Peninsula, or rather the familiar and fruitful part of it that the enemy had occupied, was divided into two administrative areas, each with its own governor: Nearer Spain to the east and north and Farther Spain to the south. The founding of the first Roman town in Spain, Itálica, the splendid ruins of which can still be visited near Seville, celebrated the completion of the victory over Carthage. The inhabitants of the Peninsula, all indiscriminately labeled Iberians by the Romans and henceforth by posterity, automatically became subjects of Rome and only too soon began to feel the weight of the conqueror's boot. High tributes in minerals and in natural products such as corn and oil had to be paid, and compulsory levies of auxiliary troops had to be provided. But worse than these were the extortions of the governors, determined to wring all they could out of the land where, according to Strabo, even the horses were reputed to feed from silver mangers. This epoch in Spain's history was certainly not a happy one. As one historian has remarked: "What the pages of the history of Rome in Spain down to the year 133 have to tell us, whether explicitly or implicitly, takes its place among the most shameful records in the whole of that history."

The outcome of the repression was, not surprisingly, wholesale revolt. It broke out in 195 amongst the peaceable Turdetani in the south —a gauge of the severity and extent of the repression—spread to Nearer Spain, and eventually set the whole Peninsula aflame. It brought Cato to Spain with a full consular army, and its continuation eventually imposed upon Rome the necessity for a system of permanent military service. The sustained ferocity of two of the outbreaks has earned them the status of full-scale wars—the Lusitanian War and the Celtiberian.

They raged more or less concurrently from 154 to 133 and at times the struggle acquired the semblance of a united national effort. On the Roman side the battle was characterized by some shameful examples of treachery and broken faith. The war with the heroically tenacious Lusitanians was in fact only brought to an end when the Roman leader engineered the murder, by two Lusitanian traitors, of their immensely gifted chieftain Viriathus—a shepherd turned bandit who eventually devoted himself to the higher cause of his country's freedom. Far more skilled in military strategy and tactics than his powerful adversaries, Viriathus had for eight years dealt the Romans one blow after another, revealing at the same time a capacity for clemency which they lacked. Equal in stature to the best of Spain's Roman opponents, he towers above most of them both as man and leader. He is Spain's first hero known to history.

Courage was not an attribute exclusive to the tribes of the far west. The warlike peoples of the interior resisted their oppressors with a dogged determination epitomized by the famous town of Numantia on the Duero River, which was immortalized by Cervantes in his play *The Siege of Numancia.* From 153 onward the settlement withstood repeated attacks by the Romans. Successive consuls came to grief on the reefs of Numantian energy and pride and had to buy peace with treaties which they soon broke. The crowning disgrace came in 137 when 20,000 Romans surrendered to a force of between 4,000 and 8,000 Numantians. The pressure exerted by a shocked Rome when this humiliation became known, resulted in the sending to Spain of Rome's greatest general, Scipio Aemilianus. He prepared to reduce Numantia by starvation. With seven camps and 60,000 men he encircled the town of only 4,000 inhabitants with a cordon so tight that escape or relief was impossible. Sixteen months later, after the Numantians' attempt to obtain honorable terms had been turned down, and after they had been driven in their desperation to suicide, Scipio burned the valiant town to the ground. In the following year Scipio gave it a supreme accolade; he chose to be known thereafter as Scipio Numantinus.

The fall of Numantia which marked the end of the Celtiberian War, was a major event in the colonization of the Peninsula. Except for Asturias and Cantabria, native resistance had effectively spent itself. The subjugation of the northwest, not fully accomplished for another

hundred years, has been described as "more a large-scale police action than a war." The wars brought about certain reforms, but in general Roman rule in Spain under the Republic continued to be characterized by its brutality. The resulting sporadic outbursts of insurrection drew to Spain some of Rome's greatest names. In 80 B.C. Quintus Sertorius, a former praetor of Nearer Spain and the son of a Roman father and Iberian mother, set up an independent government in Spain and flouted Rome as the hero of an oppressed people. Against him Rome sent Pompey, who marched through the interior, founding the city of Pamplona on the way; but Pompey's progressively successful campaigns were rendered no longer necessary in 72 by the murder of Sertorius at a banquet at Huesca. Some twenty-three years later the Peninsula became the scene of the struggle for power between Pompey and Caesar himself. That Roman dominance in one form or another was by now accepted in Spain is witnessed by the fact that Spaniards rallied to Pompey's cause. The cause was lost, however, and Caesar triumphed.

The end finally came in 19 B.C. Seven years earlier Emperor Augustus in person had initiated the reduction of Cantabria. A war-weary soldiery and a desperate enemy made the death struggle a prolonged one and Augustus was forced through illness to retire. But in 19

This Roman aqueduct, almost 2,000 years old, still supplies water for Segovia.

Agrippa was called to Spain and he succeeded in breaking the last
centers of native resistance. The two-hundred-year battle was over
and Roman Spain was a fact.

With pacification came the unhampered development of Hispania,
as the Romans had christened the Iberian Peninsula, and its integration
into the newly founded Roman Empire. After some reshuffling of territory, the Peninsula at the beginning of the Christian era consisted of
three distinct zones: Tarraconensis, by which Nearer Spain was extended to include most of central Spain, Cantabria, Asturias, and
Galicia; Baetica (Andalusia) with its boundary pushed back from the
Tagus River to the Guadiana; and Lusitania, a newly created province
that laid the geographic foundations of modern Portugal. Later on, the
Balearic Islands and Morocco were incorporated into the government
of the Peninsula, establishing thus early on Spain's claim to them.

This full-scale administrative effort was accompanied by all the civilizing benefits of rule by imperial Rome. A program of urbanization
was initiated. Towns were built to lure the recalcitrant into stability
and acquiescence with privileges that ranged from minor liberties to
the ultimate prize of Roman citizenship; and the survivors of the insurrection in the north were encouraged or compelled to settle in them.
The towns were eventually linked by a 12,000-mile network of roads,
including the mammoth Via Augusta which stretched from Cádiz
along the coast to the Pyrenees. Although originally intended as military routes these naturally contributed enormously to the economic
development of the Peninsula and to the spread of the Roman way of
life. With the towns, the aqueducts, and the amphitheaters, many
remains of which still survive today, they were the visible symbol of
a new advanced era of civilization.

After Italy Spain became one of the most productive parts of the
Roman Empire. Wines, olives, oil, and grain were exported to all parts
of the Mediterranean, and Spanish gold, silver, lead, copper, iron, and
tin poured onto the world market, with tin and lead reaching even
India. According to Pliny the annual gold output of the mines of Asturias, Galicia, and Lusitania amounted to twenty thousand pounds in
weight. As for agriculture, under the Romans the agrarian pattern of
the country, especially in the south, became one of large landed estates
(latifundia) in the hands of native leaders—now transformed into

powerful landowners—and of rich immigrants from Rome. It is a pattern that has survived in the south until this day and that has proved one of the major obstacles to Spain's agricultural well-being.

In spite of the inadequacies of Roman rule and in spite of the fact that in the north numerous tribes remained aloof until the last to the seductive benefits of the Roman machine, the truth remains that under the first period of empire Spain enjoyed a prolonged period of political stability and commercial prosperity such as she has rarely, if ever, achieved since. Peace and civilization bring their own freedoms. And inevitably, progressive Romanization and integration brought improvements. Augustus initiated the process by making the provincial governors salaried officials and by introducing reforms, such as the levying of a new general tax that distributed the burden of taxation more evenly. So great was the impact of this tax that the year in which it was introduced, 38 B.C., was taken as the dawn of a new era: until the late Middle Ages it was the point of departure for reckoning dates in Spain instead of the year of Christ's birth. The Roman legions in the Peninsula were gradually reduced, and increasing numbers of townships achieved civic emancipation. The ranks of the enslaved and the semi-free decreased with the passage of time and more men achieved the status of tenant farmer. And of course intermarriage did its work. The population of Hispania soon became a mixture of natives and part-natives, of Romans born in Rome and Romans born in Spain, a mixture so varied that the people the Visigoths would find in fifth-century Spain have to be called, for want of any more accurate term, Hispano-Romans. And this mongrel population contributed its great men to Roman history. A century after final pacification, a Spanish Roman, Trajan, became emperor, to be followed by his nephew Hadrian. Both were born in the Andalusian capital of Itálica. The two Senecas and Lucan were all three Spanish Romans from Córdoba, while the rhetorician Quintilian and the satirist Martial were not only born in Spain but were partially of native Spanish stock. The stage on which these famous men exercised their respective talents was not of course the Peninsula, but Rome itself. All roads led to Rome and all eyes were on it. There, to the very heart of the civilized world, flocked the gilded youth of its far-flung empire. Hispania remained what it had been since the conquest, a satellite of Rome.

One of the lasting bequests of Rome to the Peninsula, and one of the most powerful factors in its Romanization, was Latin itself. No subsequent occupation, however protracted, managed to usurp it in the way Anglo-Saxon usurped the Roman tongue in England. Its eventual adoption by the people as a whole is easy to understand. The pre-Roman population spoke a vast range of languages and dialects which could in no way withstand the convenience and effectiveness of a sophisticated language spoken by conquerors and settlers, by educators, administrators, and magistrates alike. Naturally, the Latin spoken in Spain was not for long Latin in its pristine state. The Latin of officialdom remained comparatively unadulterated, but the Latin of everyday life was vulgar, not classical, Latin. It was a Latin conditioned by the peculiarities of speech of uneducated soldiers and of settlers and traders from different parts of the Roman world, and not least by the natural wayward development of a language deprived of direct contact with its life source. It was a Latin, moreover, colored by the vocabulary and habits of pronunciation of the languages it overlaid. It was

With Christianity came ritual and heavenly personae to engage the artist's imagination. Above is a highly stylized manuscript illumination of angels.

a Latin which centuries of evolution were to turn into the romance tongues of the Peninsula in the way that the Latin of Italy became Italian and the Latin of Gaul French.

The empire's other permanent gift to Spain was Christianity, which reached the Mediterranean coasts in the middle of the first century. As had happened before in the case of new ideas and new cultures, it was initially in the cities of the south and east that the Gospel prospered. In the interior the new religion had to fight a hard battle with pagan superstition and religiosity. But gradually the influence of "Old Spain" imposed itself. The repressions suffered by Christians in the second and third centuries struck a sympathetic chord among a people who, like Roman subjects everywhere, were feeling the effects of the increasing authoritarianism of an empire in decline. Christianity was the religion of the poor and the downtrodden, and as extortion and rapacity once more became the characteristics of Roman rule, increasing numbers of the Peninsula's inhabitants were thrust into destitution and found themselves forced to sell themselves into slavery. Spain, therefore, contributed its share of martyrs to the Christian-thirsty State. Indeed it was a Spaniard, Emperor Theodosius, who in 380 made Christianity the empire's official religion and denounced adherents of other faiths as heretics to be punished; and it was in Spain that three of the Church's most important early councils establishing dogma and discipline took place. These facts are strangely prophetic of the unique nature of Spain's subsequent relationship with Christianity and the Church.

Ironically, as the threatening rumble of the barbarian world outside grew louder—between the years 264 and 276 the Peninsula was devastated by Franks and Suevi—and the very foundations of the edifice of Rome began to crumble, the Church succeeded its former enemy the State as the source and symbol of stability in a hostile and chaotic world. With the growth of Christianity, Spain began to develop a certain consciousness of itself as a thing apart from the Roman Empire, a certain sense of separate identity, and as the empire disintegrated the Church played an increasingly larger role in secular as well as religious life. When the end came, Roman Spain, disillusioned with, and impervious to, a decayed and weakened Rome, succumbed with hardly a struggle. But in one lasting sense the empire survived. As a state-oriented hierarchical and authoritarian organization patterned on Rome, the Church outlived and at the same time perpetuated the organism that helped produce it. It imposed itself upon the heresies of the invaders and provided the Peninsula with its strongest source of continuity throughout the upheavals of the long centuries to come.

In A.D. 409 the Germanic hordes poured across the Pyrenees into a terrified and defeated Spain. Ironically, the peoples from the north were to all intents and purposes Rome's guests. The Alans, the Suevi, and the Vandals were invited into Spain by a general of the empire making his own personal bid for power. In order to oust these tribes, the Romans in 418 signed a pact with the Visigoths, another Germanic people who, during the fifth century operated in the south of France, ostensibly as an army of Roman auxiliaries. The Visigoths were to be granted lands in Aquitaine in exchange for restoring the three Hispanic provinces to Rome. They did indeed drive the Suevi into far Galicia, defeat the Alans, and oust the Vandals from Andalusia, to which they gave their name. But the Visigoths also, in the absence of effective control from Rome, established themselves as Spain's new governors.

In the midst of the Peninsula's estimated six million inhabitants the 200,000 Visigoths with their long hair and massive jewelry were a mere handful. They established their capital at Toledo, for the first time making the center, rather than the older periphery, the focus of the Peninsula. And there in the center they remained, a caste apart from the mass of the population, an aristocratic and military elite hardly affected even by the eventual removal of the ban on mixed marriages. As a direct consequence of this social and geographical isolation, the language of the Peninsula remained Vulgar Latin, and the invaders, far from imposing their own tongue on the inhabitants they found there, themselves became the victims of a linguistic imposition. They had to content themselves with contributing a mere few hundred words to the language of their adoption.

It is now realized that the Visigothic era in Spain, rather than significantly changing the development of the Peninsula in any way, must be regarded for the most part as an "appendix" to the six-hundred-year rule of Rome. The economic and social tendencies of Spain under the late empire continued, becoming simply more marked. The Visigoths being first a military and then a land-oriented people, the process of deurbanization was accelerated. The bourgeoisie that Roman rule had brought into being in Spain, and then proceeded to undermine, was virtually extinguished. Industry continued to decline and Mediterranean trade was severely affected. Roman coinage remained the only currency until the reign of King Leovigild (569–586). The sole major contribution made to the pattern of peninsular economy by the Visigoths seems to have been their predilection for herding animals. They appear to have been initially responsible for the development of the transmigratory flock as the very core of Spain's agrarian policy, at the cost—the enormous cost as it was to transpire centuries later—of a prosperous agriculture. The Visigothic era, in fact, marks a period of transition between the flourishing mercantile economy of Roman rule in its heyday and the rural domestic economy of the early Middle Ages.

The Visigothic takeover was by any standards a speedy and painless affair, but they did not continue to have things entirely their own way. Pressure from encroaching Franks in the north, from resurgent Suevi in the northwest, and from Byzantium in the south and east, for years kept the Visigothic armies on the march, until the great Leovigild succeeded in establishing Visigothic supremacy after A.D. 569.

The greatest source of disruption, however, was not an outside, hostile world, but the Visigothic elite itself. The monarchical system that they introduced into Spain and which for the first time, in theory at least, made the Peninsula a nation in its own right instead of a collection of tribes or a mere Roman province, was elective, not hereditary. This system, forged by the conditions of a military, nomadic life, proved totally inadequate for the requirements of a stable government and society. Every noble was his king's peer and therefore capable and desirous of succeeding him. The result was constant upheaval at the very summit of society. Sensitive to the full charisma of monarchy, Leovigild was the first Spanish king to wear a crown, to sit on a throne, and to have coins minted in his image, and he obtained a token acceptance of the idea of a hereditary monarchy from his nobles. But within the space of a few reigns, the innovation collapsed.

If the monarchy was a continuous source of instability and unrest, the Christian Church increasingly became a source of power and strength. The Church's career can indeed be seen as the victory of Hispano-Roman Spain over the Visigothic intrusion. The Visigoths,

of course, had been already converted to Christianity before their arrival in Spain and had possessed the Bible in their own Germanic tongue. They were, however, adherents of the Eastern heresy of Arianism, which denied the Trinity, while the Hispano-Romans were staunchly Catholic and solidly remained so. Catholicism eventually triumphed. But it was a triumph achieved only through the bitter expediency of civil war. Leovigild's son, Hermenegild, married a Catholic, was converted by her, and then rose in rebellion against his father. His five-year struggle ended in failure. Hermenegild was murdered by his jailer when he refused to abjure and became the first Visigothic martyr. However, his elder brother, Reccared—a more subtle man—had learned much from the protracted battle put up by the Hispano-Romans of the south. Realizing that only a Catholic would ever command the loyalty of the mass of the people, he announced his own conversion a year after his succession to the throne. Two years later in 589 Catholicism was made the official faith of the Peninsula.

Catholic Christianity had become the state religion of Spain, and out of the ensuing alliance between Church and Crown the Church as

The Christian Visigoths retained a barbarian taste for brilliant adornments such as these bejeweled gilt bronze fibulae.

a secular power was born. Bishops were incorporated into the royal council and soon played their part in elections to the Crown. The Church's contribution, however, was not merely a political one. As well as providing Visigothic Spain with its two intellectual giants— Saint Leander and his more famous brother Saint Isidore, both arch- bishops of Seville—the clergy gave definitive form to the State as a legislative entity. Visigoths and Hispano-Romans were for the first two hundred years subject to their own laws, Germanic or Roman. Then in the middle of the seventh century the task of legislative uni- fication was undertaken under King Chindaswinth. The result, the *Liber Judiciorum*—or *Fuero Juzgo* as it was later called in Castilian— was promulgated by his son Recceswinth in 654. Whether the code's primary debt is to Germanic customary law or to Roman law is still a subject for debate, but the traces of Visigothic attitudes—their concept of honor and personal vengeance, the personal relationship of over- lord-serf, the anti-Semitism—are undeniably and predictably apparent. The code, which has left its mark on Spanish life and literature, is in fact the lasting monument to the Visigothic state. Some of its pro- visions remained law for centuries.

In spite of the achievements of the Church, Visigothic Spain failed ultimately to become a working reality. Like oil and water the Visi- gothic aristocracy and the Hispanic population stubbornly refused to mix, and the social and ethnic contradictions on which the ship of state gingerly floated rendered it a fragile vessel indeed. It foundered finally in the turbulent waters of that aristocratic anarchy which the monarchy had proved unable to quell. King Witiza, who like former sovereigns had tried to control the succession, had shared the throne with his son Achila. But upon Witiza's death in 710, the nobles elected a king of their own choice, Roderick, and provoked Achila into rebel- lion. Civil strife of this sort was a familiar accompaniment to the death of kings, but this time events followed a course which led to one of the major milestones in the Peninsula's history.

Count Julian, the governor of the Spanish outpost of Ceuta on the Moroccan coast, joined the battle against Roderick and enlisted Arab aid from North Africa. In 711 an African Berber army of 7,000 under their leader Tarik landed on the prominence called thenceforth the Rock of Tarik (Gebel Tarik, or Gibraltar). In the ensuing Battle of

Guadalete, near Jerez de la Frontera, the invaders brought Visigothic
rule in Spain crashing down. Roderick disappeared in the battle, leaving behind his white horse with its saddle of gilded buckskin adorned with rubies and emeralds, his gold mantle embroidered with pearls and rubies, and one silver shoe. The Church appears to have played an ignominious part in the Visigoths' defeat. One of the wings of Roderick's army which went over to the enemy was commanded by the archbishop of Seville, a brother of the late Witiza. His motives were obviously purely political, but unwittingly he betrayed his country and his religion to Islam. For, hardly surprisingly, the Moslems summoned in the name of political expediency would not be so readily conjured back across the Strait of Gibraltar once their job was done.

In less than a century Islam had steam-rollered its way from Arabia to Africa's Atlantic shores. The legendarily rich land eight miles across the Mediterranean to the north was an obvious outlet for its religious and expansionist zeal, and almost certainly in its relentless spread it would have arrived there in any case. As it was, once invited over, the Moslems had no intention of returning. With ease they overran the greater part of a country which had withstood the might of Rome for two centuries but which now felt no political allegiance to its former masters. Nearly eight hundred years were to pass before the whole of the Peninsula was wrested from their grasp.

The legend that surrounds the doom of the Visigothic Spain is far more romantic than the reality. King Roderick, it goes, one day took by force the beautiful daughter of Count Julian as she bathed in the Tagus in Toledo. Her father, answering her messages for help, arrived to take her home to Africa. As they left, the king, unaware that his crime was known, asked Julian to send him a certain breed of hawk from Africa. The count agreed, promising to send hawks such as the king never dreamed of. Shortly afterward the "hawks" landed in Spain —Count Julian had opened the floodgates to Islam in vengeance for his dishonor.

Romance or reality, the implication is the same—Visigothic Spain carried within itself the seeds of its defeat. There could have been no more apt relic of Spain's Visigothic period—outwardly splendid but inwardly soft and insecure—than Roderick's mislaid silver slipper.

CHAPTER II

THE ADVENT
OF ISLAM

"**Y**ou must know how the Grecian maidens, as handsome as houris, their necks glittering with innumerable pearls and jewels, their bodies clothed with tunics of costly silks and sprinkled with gold, are awaiting your arrival, reclining on soft couches in the sumptuous palaces of crowned lords and princes. . . . You know that the great lords of the island are willing to make you their sons and brethren by marriage."

So spoke the Arab commander to his troops on the eve of their first departure for Spain, revealing how the legend of the golden land of the Biblical Tarshish still survived. Little wonder with such a glorious prize to be won that in 712 the first invading force under Tarik was joined by the Arab governor of the African Maghreb, Musa ibn-Nusayr, and a large contingent of Arabs. Between them they set about subduing the Peninsula. Some cities resisted and many Christians fled to Gaul or to the mountains of Cantabria, but many more were content to live on under the new regime, and by 718 the country had fallen like a ripe plum into the hands of the caliph of Damascus, then capital of the Islamic world. Following the example of Musa's son, who took Rod-

Thirteenth-century Moslem horsemen celebrate the end of Ramadan.

erick's widow to wife, the invaders married into Spain as they had been promised, and settled down eagerly in the country whose natural delights and monuments of civilization—the bequest of Rome—contrasted so favorably with the desert from which many of them had come. They settled without attempting to colonize in the Roman fashion, or to centralize as the Visigoths had tried to do; and the natives for their part were more than content to relapse once more into their old separatist ways. Local autonomy under Moslem protection was a not uncommon compromise, suiting as it did so well the needs or demands of both sides. The fact that after enjoying the status of an independent kingdom they had been relegated once more to the position of a colony or province of a distant empire, was not one to worry the mass of the people.

The Islamic impetus did not come to a halt in Spain. When their victory in the Peninsula was more or less complete, the Moslems continued their drive northward into France. They penetrated as far as Poitiers, only to be routed there in 732 by the armies of Charles Martel. France, and perhaps much more of Europe, was thereby saved for Christendom, and the Moslems were driven back beyond the Pyrenees. Thenceforth they contented themselves with al-Andalus, as they called Islamic Spain. Such was their lack of concern for any program of thorough colonization that they even left to its own devices that wild, unwelcoming corner of the mountainous north which had always remained invincible and to which a number of the more recalcitrant elements of the Visigothic regime had fled when their monarch fell. Had Cantabria too been acquired for Islam, the Reconquest might never have materialized.

Although Islam was conceived by its founder Mohammed and its members as a community of believers all of whom were equal before the law—a tenet of faith that militated against a Spanish feudalism— and although the duty of every adherent was militant proselytization, the Moslems adopted a policy of religious toleration. The fact that Christianity too possessed a Holy Book and that it shared many features with Mohammedanism helped justify this policy, but there was as well a concrete benefit to be gained by the rulers—the revenue derived from the poll tax levied upon all who chose to remain Christians. Undoubtedly it was the lure of exemption from this tax that effected the conversion to Islam of many thousands of Christians. Within three centuries, Spain indeed was a country with a Moslem majority, the peasants to the south of the Duero in the west and to the south of the Pyrenees in the east having become Mohammedans.

Nevertheless, in spite of the advantages of apostasy, large communities of Christians living under Moslem rule remained true to their beliefs. These Mozarabs, as they were called, who were for the greater part urban dwellers, spoke Arabic as well as their own Vulgar Latin and in many respects adapted themselves to the Islamic way of life, while remaining Christians. Living in isolation from what remained of Christian Spain, they developed an art, culture, and poetry distinctively their own. The Mozarabic rite remained untouched by the successive innovations of its Roman counterpart and is still celebrated today in Toledo Cathedral. Mozarabic Spanish acquired its own linguistic peculiarities. By bridging the gap between the two communities the Mozarabs formed a group of enormous significance to the way in which this country of two cultures and two religions developed. (The Mudejars, a smaller group of Moslems living within Christianized regions of Spain, would never achieve comparable influence.)

The fact that the settlers from Africa were not simply the Moors (North Africans) that tradition has indifferently accredited them with being, but a mixture of Arab leaders, Coptic sailors, and Syrian as well as Berber warriors, brought with it its own complications. Sectarian differences and Moslem family feuds did not in these early years make for harmony at such a distance from the central authority at Damascus, and the tendency of the Arabs to claim for themselves the fertile, civilized south, leaving the grim central lands to their Berber underlings, merely intensified the struggle over the spoils of conquest. In Damascus itself the Arab proclivity for family rivalry exploded in 750 into upheaval at the very summit of the power structure, with the reigning line, the Umayyads, being ousted by their opponents the Abbasids. The sole survivor of the ruling family, a boy of nineteen, succeeded eventually in making his way to al-Andalus which had for the most part supported the Umayyad dynasty, and in 756 he entered the capital Córdoba as Islamic Spain's acclaimed new leader, Abd-al-Rahman I. Though still of Islam, the province had become an independent emirate, to all intents and purposes free of the

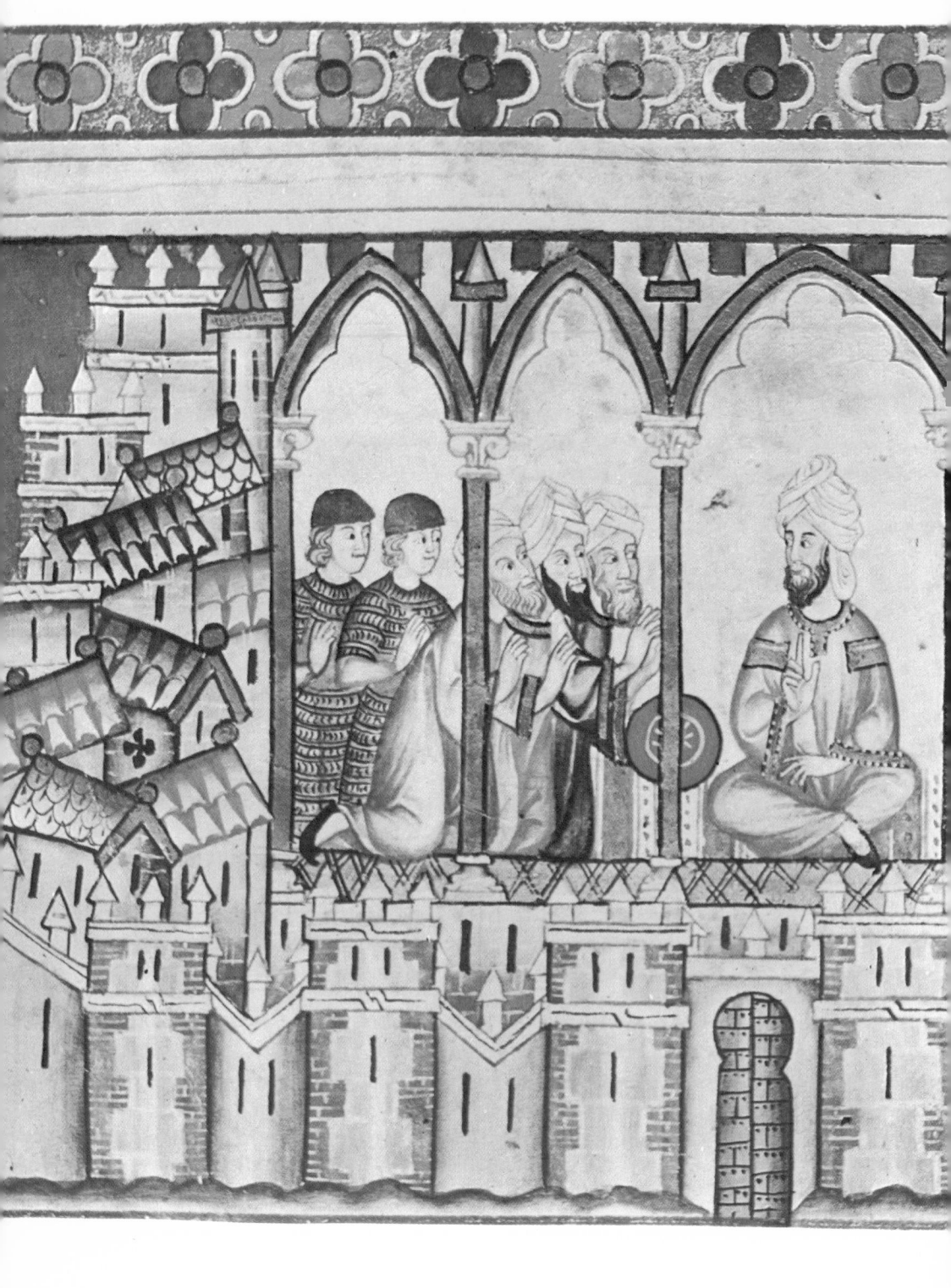

central authority, which had meanwhile removed from Damascus to Baghdad. The emirate did not embrace the whole of the Peninsula, however, though it occupied the lion's share. The area around Saragossa in the northeast had made itself virtually independent of the south by establishing a separate Moslem government in the city, while farther to the west the devastations of a five-year famine had driven the Berbers from the territory bounded by Coimbra on the west, Toledo on the south, Pamplona on the northeast, and the Christian-occupied mountains on the north.

In spite of the comparative ease with which he succeeded to power, Abd-al-Rahman's reign was not a trouble-free one. Rather his authority became the focus of the revolts and struggles for power that had hitherto followed a more haphazard pattern. Abd-al-Rahman's answer was the creation of a permanent army which included forty thousand Berbers and Slavs from southern Europe, but this military regime, although perpetuated by his successors, did not manage to inhibit the constant mushrooming of revolts in the reigns that followed. As far as the Christian north was concerned, of course, nothing was more to its advantage than an al-Andalus too preoccupied with internal conflict to notice or care what was happening amongst the bands of shepherds in Cantabria.

These hill people were not biding their time for a grand offensive against the "infidel." But, fiercely independent as they always had been, they continued to harass alien settlements, farms, travelers, and armies. More important, in the face of Moslem neglect, they started slowly to encroach territorially upon the no man's land that separated them from Islamic civilization to the south. Since their life was primarily a pastoral one, this gradual takeover of wider expanses of land did not entail the settlement difficulties of land husbandry: advance and retreat were equally viable.

In spite of conflict within, hostility from without, and constant irritation on its borders, the emirate of al-Andalus managed to prosper and progress. Contacts with the East were eventually renewed, opening the door to that flowering of activity which was to make tenth-century Moslem Spain the cultural and intellectual center of a still-benighted Europe, a glittering meteor of civilization in a sky that was empty of all but a few stars. When the Arabs burst out of Arabia in the seventh

A Moslem governor of Seville holds a war council in his castle, the alcazar.

century they had been a nomadic people, on the whole rude and illiterate. The countries they overran, however, were many of them the scene of ancient and highly developed civilizations, and their own empire expanded until it bordered on two greater ones, Persia on the east and Byzantium on the west. The Arabs themselves became primarily imitators and transmitters, rather than creators, and herein lies their unique contribution to European civilization. Their appetite for culture and knowledge was insatiable, their willingness to adopt and adapt that with which they came into contact, complete. From the East and from Byzantium they absorbed a great deal and it was they who preserved for and passed on to the West much of the culture and literature of Persia, India, and Greece. And the principal clearinghouse for this momentous transaction was Spain. Islamic Spain, as well as creating its own distinctive culture on the basis of what Islam brought its way, served as the channel for the transmission of knowledge from civilized East to "barbarian" West, as the stage on which the Dark Ages yielded before the growing light shed by the dawn of a new era.

Al-Andalus was particularly blessed in these early centuries by having as its leaders emirs who were themselves men of culture and learning. In the ninth century under Abd-al-Rahman II, al-Andalus

Moorish architecture, with its decorated plasterwork and inlaid materials, has left an exotic stamp on such cities as Granada, Córdoba, and Seville.

entered the first phase of its prosperity. It had its own navy of some three hundred vessels, as well as a standing army. A truce was made with the Christian north and the emir entered upon full diplomatic relations with the Byzantine Empire. Not least, the economic boom that made the country rich and gave solid foundation to its cultural flowering got under way.

One or two significant differences apart, the economic face of Moslem Spain continued in general to have much the same physiognomy as before, though at a much higher level of success than in Visigothic times and even perhaps than in the heyday of Roman rule. The pattern of land distribution in the rich and fertile south altered hardly at all. Whether in the hands of indigenous or Arab overlords, the old large-estate system, introduced by the Romans and perpetuated by the Visigoths, survived virtually intact. Where the actual cultivation of the soil was concerned, however, the Moslems introduced their own sharecrop system, adopted from the Byzantines. This differed from the European feudal norm in that it was based on an agricultural contract between two free men, and meant that the men who worked the land were unquestionably better off under Moslem rule than they had been under the Visigoths. Trade with the Near East, with North

Africa, and above all with the Christian north, flourished, as al-Andalus exported its textiles, oil, and weapons in all directions and imported for its own people, and hence for Europe as a whole, the spices and luxury goods of the East. The skilled artisan classes, who were mostly Mozarabic, learned much from the exotic produce that entered their country from the Orient and on this foundation created an immensely varied and highly prosperous craft economy, producing pottery, silks, decorated leathers, bookbindings, enameled and inscribed weapons, carved ivory, enameled glass, and precious wrought metalwork which became the coveted prizes of the rich of Europe.

If the Mozarabs, together with the entrepreneurial Jews (who flourished under Islam after the black days of Visigothic anti-Semitism), were largely responsible for the highly developed trade in consumer goods, most, if not all, of the credit for al-Andalus' thriving agriculture must go to the Moslems. They cultivated the land and, exploiting and perfecting the Roman techniques already used in the Peninsula and those of the Near East which they introduced there, made the southern and eastern regions into a fertile, well-irrigated garden of fruit orchards, sugar-cane and rice fields, olive groves, vineyards, and cereal farms. Valuing nature's cornucopia as only a people with desert memories can, they even planted groves of oaks and pines—a farsighted commercial enterprise indeed. A living testimony to the contribution made by Spanish Moslems to the life and economy of the Peninsula is that a large proportion of the four thousand Arabic words found in the Spanish language refer to agricultural produce and techniques and to commerce in general.

The effects that this robust economic life had upon the Christian kingdoms in the north were mixed. Trade between north and south was understandably brisk and contributed to the amicable compromise that for long periods characterized relations between the two parts of Spain. The rough north could not, did not wish to, withstand the benefits that the civilized south could bestow. These benefits, paradoxically, increased with the beginnings of religious intolerance.

In the ninth and tenth centuries, as the tolerant era began to give way to one of repression, large numbers of Mozarabs who doggedly resisted conversion emigrated north and established themselves in León and Castile. Naturally they took with them—as well as an in-

grained antagonism toward Islam—their way of life, their crafts, and
their experience of life in a prosperous, stable society, thus introducing
a note of sophistication into their new environment. The ebb and flow
of war over the centuries had a similar effect. Any territorial advances
made by the Moslems washed their civilization a little farther north,
while the steady push southward of the Christians absorbed land
where the Moslem way of life had for long been the norm. Though
al-Andalus in these ways enriched the Christian kingdoms from without, at the same time it inhibited development within. For the trade
was largely one way. Not only did the territorial imperative distract
Christian society from developing a stable society on a strong economic
basis, but the very presence next door of such an economy made it
unnecessary. An indication of this reliance is that for nearly four hundred years the only coinage used in the north was Arabic or French.

Abd-al-Rahman II, with his love of philosophy, astrology, medicine,
astronomy, music, and poetry—the study of which he actively encouraged at his court—had a fitting sense of the emergent greatness of
his nation. He filled Córdoba with splendid buildings and extended
the great mosque built by his predecessor on the site of the Visigothic
church of Saint Vincent's. It was under Abd-al-Rahman III, however,
that Córdoba became the bejeweled center of the Moslem world.

This Abd-al-Rahman, who had Navarrese blood in his veins and
whose hair was light enough to warrant his dying it black, came to
power in 912 at the age of twenty-one, and seventeen years later in 929
he took the audacious step of proclaiming himself caliph and al-
Andalus no longer an emirate but a caliphate independent of Baghdad.
These seventeen years he had spent in asserting upon Moslem Spain
an effective central authority such as it had rarely if ever experienced.
And once the last centers of resistance, Toledo, Badajoz, and Saragossa
(by now representing more or less the northernmost boundaries of
al-Andalus), had capitulated, this greatest of Spain's Moslem rulers
turned his attention to the steadily encroaching Christian north and
the question of security.

This did not mean he had no time for the pleasures and delights of
this life—always compatible in the Mohammedan vision of man's
existence with the higher matters of the spirit—and his capital became
the tangible symbol of a way of living that was rich, civilized, and

OVERLEAF: *A barren stretch of countryside in the province of Valladolid*

sensuous. At a time when other capitals of Europe were still little more than haphazard agglomerations of primitive mansions, squalid hovels, filthy streets, and the occasional church—and indeed were long to remain so—Córdoba was a great city of patios, gardens, fountains, grand palaces, and gracious houses, with at least four hundred mosques, nine hundred public baths, and no fewer than seventy libraries. Its streets were paved with stone, and hundreds of lamps, many made of silver, hung from the columns of the larger temples. Little wonder that Córdoba became the exotic focus of a bedazzled Europe, the place where many a northern ruler might apply in search of expertise or excellence, whether he was in need of a surgeon, an architect, or a singing master.

Though the Christian kings in northern Spain, like their counterparts in other countries, looked to the Moslem south for the civilized adornments of life, and in their case even imitated such habits as the wearing of flowing Arab apparel and sitting at floor level on cushions, this in no way affected their firm commitment to a policy of southward expansion. And when necessary, military alliances were formed with resurgent Moslems, with the Mozarabs of Toledo and the *Muladíes* (converts to Islam) of Saragossa.

Abd-al-Rahman, however, was a warrior of energy as well as a ruler of distinction, and in retaliation for these fifth-column activities within his gates, he led two expeditions against the Christians: one against Navarre, whose capital, Pamplona, was sacked and whose cathedral was completely destroyed by fire; the other against León. Navarre he succeeded in making into a tribute state. Spurred on by these successes, in 939 he launched a "campaign of omnipotence," as he called it, against Asturias, in an attempt to destroy its southern frontier at Zamora and assert his authority over the Peninsula as a whole. But this time fate did not smile on the Moslems. His army of ten thousand was routed by the Christians before the city of Simancas, and Abd-al-Rahman himself was driven to the indignity of flight, leaving behind him on the battlefield the Koran that was amongst his most treasured possessions and his coat of gilded mail. In an attempt to soothe his hurt pride he had several hundred officers crucified for cowardice.

The situation was for the time being one of stalemate. By his death in 961, however, Abd-al-Rahman had managed to exact tribute from each of the northern kingdoms in turn. Unable to defeat them outright in spite of their constant internecine warring, he settled for a system of vassalage to his own empire. It was an expedient which the Christians likewise found convenient in the centuries that followed.

When the long reign of Abd-al-Rahman III came to an end, Moslem power was supreme again in the Peninsula. He had established beyond question the authority of his house, imposing unity upon his own subjects as well as vassalage upon the Christian kingdoms in the north. Furthermore, he had asserted the sway of the caliphate of al-Andalus upon North Africa, by seizing Ceuta and gradually securing the submission of all the independent Berber tribes. In the process he had made of Moslem Spain a power feared and respected throughout Europe and the Near East, a power to which all countries that came within its orbit, including Germany, Italy, and Byzantium, sent their ambassadors. To his glittering capital of Córdoba there came at his invitation Greek and Byzantine artists and architects. In its libraries were collected the Greek and Latin manuscripts that Moslem Spain preserved for the West. Gathered there also were the Greek scholars, sent for at his request, who, in collaboration with resident Moslems and Jews, translated these valuable Greek writings into Arabic against the day when they would eventually be turned into Latin and become fully accessible to Europe. Under this dynamic, stocky, blue-eyed Spanish Umayyad, Moslem Spain was at its zenith, reaching heights of power, influence, consolidated authority, prosperity, and civilization which it would never again simultaneously enjoy. No subsequent caliph rivaled the mighty stature of the first.

While the prestige of the caliphate after Abd-al-Rahman III was sustained by its own momentum, it failed to retain the vitality with which its founder had imbued it. Abd-al-Rahman's son, who married a Basque, was a semi-invalid whose major accomplishment was the accumulation and annotation of something like four hundred thousand books—no mean feat in an age when few rulers could even read, but not the sort of exclusivist preoccupation that makes for effective political control. As the caliph contentedly led his hermetic scholar's life, the situation became ripe for a bid for power from beneath, and when al-Hakam II died in 976 leaving as heir the twelve-year-old Hisham II, that bid materialized in the formidable person of Muhammad ibn-abi-

Amir, later known as al-Mansur, the Queen Mother's favorite and the second outstanding political and military figure of Spanish Islam.

The greatest warrior that Moslem Spain ever produced, al-Mansur ("the Victorious") with the help of his Berber levies effectively ruled al-Andalus for over twenty years. Although known as the "scourge of the Christians," his prestige was so great that he counted among his wives the daughters of no lesser personages than the kings of León and Navarre—a fact that eloquently illustrates the complex and ambiguous relations between north and south. A harsh and ruthless man, he relentlessly ravaged the Christian territories until his very name struck terror into the hearts of their inhabitants. Al-Mansur attacked the pulse centers of the northern kingdoms, sacking Coimbra, León, Zamora, Simancas, Burgos, and even Barcelona in the far northeast. The greatest outrage of all, however, was the sack in 997 of the religious capital of Christian Spain, Santiago de Compostela, which housed the shrine of Saint James. The cathedral he razed to the ground and its great bells he took back with him to Córdoba. The deed was typical of the man. He was a destroyer rather than a creator, content to sack, pillage, and lay waste rather than to settle, harness, or absorb. He and his Berbers passed over the northern lands like a horde of locusts, leaving desert and desolation behind them. With feeling did a Christian chronicler refer to his death and "burial in hell" in 1002.

Al-Mansur's dictatorship marked a period of military glory for the south. But it also undermined the caliphate it had sought to render strong. Al-Mansur had risen to supremacy by removing all power from the Arab aristocracy and by enlisting the aid of large numbers of Berber troops. He remained at the top by relying on the support of a spy network that corroded the fabric of court life. But at least he never made the mistake of claiming titular power. His son, Sanchul did, persuading the by now middle-aged, ineffectual Caliph Hisham to name him his heir. Thus, at one stroke Sanchul set all the Arab elements in Spain against himself. While he was away in the north fighting Christians, civil war broke out at home. After twenty ignominious years, with Arabs fighting Berbers, Umayyads struggling for survival, interference from foreign mercenaries, and murder the commonest resort in successive bids for power, the caliphate collapsed and Córdoba declared itself an oligarchical republic.

The fall of the caliphate was by no means the end of Moslem Spain.
Indeed the two centuries that followed were in some ways amongst the
most remarkable in Moslem Spanish history. But they were not years
characterized by political unity and this period was thus to become
the crucial turning point in the fortunes of the Christian north. City
after city followed the example of Córdoba until al-Andalus became
a collection of some twenty-six splinter states under "party kings," the
reyes de taifa as they are called in Spanish. These city-states warred
against one another as often as they did against the Christians, and
their quarrels allowed the armies from the north to sweep down and
repay the Moslems in kind for the devastations of al-Mansur. Córdoba,
Seville, and Granada were raided in turn, and increasingly the *taifa*
kingdoms, especially along the frontier, were forced to protect themselves by accepting vassalage to Castile. The great blow, however, fell
in 1086, when the first great Moslem city to be captured permanently by
the Christians capitulated. The fact that the city was Toledo, the ancient
Visigothic capital, made this the first real milestone in the Reconquest.
In accordance with the climate of tolerance that still prevailed for the
most part in the Peninsula, the inhabitants were promised religious
freedom and given the choice of either remaining in their city or leaving it for the south.

The end of religious tolerance was, however, in sight. At the instigation of those who saw the growing Christian ascendancy as evidence
of Allah's displeasure with a people that had departed from the path
of purity and orthodoxy, the *taifa* states looked for help in their pre-
dicament to the shores of Africa. The king of Seville for one decided
that he would "rather tend the camels of the Almoravides than graze
swine in Castile." The Almoravides ("vowed to God") were a con-
federation of Saharan peoples recently converted to Islam who had
made Morocco the center of a new, fanatical Moslem kingdom, and to
these uncivilized tribesmen the once proud caliphate was driven to appeal for aid. The Almoravides required no second invitation to launch
a military crusade. In 1086 their army under their leader Yusuf ibn-
Tashfin landed in Algeciras, and by 1110 the whole of Moslem Spain
formed part of a vast empire centered in Morocco, whose southern
limits reached Senegal.

The Almoravides' religious zeal, however, did not long survive their

rise to power either in the Peninsula or in North Africa. And in North Africa they eventually succumbed to another Moslem movement, that of the even more fanatical Almohades ("unitarians"). When al-Andalus once again fell prey to the disease of civil revolt, history repeated itself and in 1145 the second wave of Berber fanatics were invited into Spain. Like the first they stayed to conquer and once again al-Andalus became one in its subjection to North Africa.

These invasions by African peoples untouched by the civilizations of the Eastern and Western Caliphates represent a turning point in the relations between the two Spains. They introduced the specter of religious persecution at a time when the Christian kingdoms were becoming increasingly conscious of their identity as heirs to a pre-Moslem past and increasingly confident about their ability to vindicate their inheritance. It was a time too when Europe was developing a certain sensitivity about the "outrage" of the continuing Moslem presence on European soil. The religious element apart, however, the new influx of Moslems was racially and socially distinctive. With the passage of time and intermarriage, the people of al-Andalus had to a large degree become Spaniards, albeit Moslem Spaniards, to their Christian fellow-countrymen. The Almoravides and the Almohades, on the other hand, were distinctly alien. Especially strange were the Black troops among them, and their war drums, perhaps the first heard in western Europe, struck terror into the hearts of the Christian adversaries, as Spain's great epic, the *Cantar de mío Cid,* written probably around the end of the twelfth century, tells us. And although they too, knowing no other home, were eventually absorbed into the ethnic fabric of southern Spain, the crucial factor is that they appeared in the Peninsula at a time when the Christian north was girding its racial and religious loins. They patently had no right to be there and the dependence on them of the Moslem Spaniards of the south cast doubts on the legitimacy of their claim too. The Berbers' arrival in Spain was the catalyst that turned the territorial advance southward of the Christian north into what might properly be termed a Reconquest and eventually a Crusade.

The irony of the two Berber dynasties is that they coincided with the highest development of Spanish Moslem and Spanish Jewish thought —with the high peak, in other words, of medieval Spanish philosophy. The Almohades as a religious group were committed to the twofold

A Moslem battle standard of gold and silver silk was made in Fez for an expedition against the Christian kings of Spain in 1340.

idea of the unity and the complete spiritualization of God, and their leader ibn-Tumart was himself a theologian. The Almoravides, or "black puritans" as they have been called, were intolerant of unorthodox thinking, though this did not deter the polymath ibn-Bajja of Saragossa, or Avempace as he is better known, from preaching his philosophy of the rational, contemplative life, in communion with the supreme intellect that was God. The same path was followed by ibn-Tufayl, who practiced medicine at Granada and whose thinking reflected the policy of the Almohad rulers: philosophical probing could be allowed to the educated, as long as the mass of people were not disturbed in the comfort of their religious faith. But the greatest contribution to philosophy of Moslem Spain was made by ibn-Rushd, or Averroës, as his Spanish name is styled, who was born in Córdoba in 1126. Using those Arabic and Latin translations of ancient works commissioned by the tenth-century Caliph Abd-al-Rahman III, Averroës discovered Aristotle, wrote commentaries on his works, and effectively reintroduced Aristotelianism—an Aristotelianism admittedly somewhat influenced by Averroës' inability to refer to the original Greek—into Europe.

The contribution of the Spanish Jews was, possibly, even greater. If al-Andalus preserved Europe's Greek heritage for the Middle Ages, it was largely the Spanish Jews who transmitted it. The great liberating event in the development of Spain's role as intermediary between East and West had occurred in 1085 with the capture of Toledo, for in the course of the following centuries, the city, now Christian but for almost four centuries a stronghold of Moslem and Mozarab civilization, became the center of a school of translators who busied themselves turning the Arabic-encased accumulated lore of Greece and the East, as well as of Moslem Spain, into the Latin of medieval Christendom. Persian and Indian literature—an important influence on early Spanish literature—Greek science and philosophy, mathematics and astronomy, botany and medicine, even chess, were among the contributions to the treasure chest of European learning; and the mainstay of the Toledan school of scholars were the learned Jews who lived and worked there. Even so, the part played by the Hispano-Jews was not merely a secondhand one. They likewise had their philosophers— Rabbi Ben Ezra, for example, who in his wanderings reputedly reached

Averroës, the twelfth-century Cordoban physician and philosopher, anachronistically discussing dietary laws with Porphyry, a third-century Greek

London, and Solomon ben-Gabirol, or Avicebron, who in his treatise
Fons vitae introduced neo-Platonism into Spain. Jewish indeed was the
thinker regarded by some as the greatest philosopher Spain has ever
produced: Moses ben-Maimon, corrupted by the Latin-speaking world
into the more famous Maimonides. Like Averroës he was born in
Córdoba and like Averroës he held that there was no real dichotomy
between reason and faith, between science and philosophy, or philosophy and religion. His influence on the great Paris-trained theologian
of the medieval Christian Church, Saint Thomas Aquinas, was considerable, in spite of the fact that Saint Thomas' *Summa contra gentiles*
was written largely in answer to what he considered the wrong thinking
of the Moslem and Jewish philosophers of Spain.

Politically and militarily the new African regime enjoyed a modest
success for a half a century or so. By the 1170s al-Andalus was completely subdued. The Berbers made the occasional treaty with one or
another of the Christian states, which still squabbled among them-

selves, and they won one great victory against the north—the Battle of Alarcos in 1195, from which the Castilian king barely escaped with his life. These years, however, were by way of being the lull before the storm, and there had already been highly significant straws in the gathering wind. As early as 1158, a Cistercian-inspired crusade had been called which led to the founding of first one, and then two more monastic societies of knights: the military orders of Calatrava, Alcántara, and Santiago, created in direct response to the Berber threat. Even before that, forces of foreign crusaders from the north had taken part in the various enterprises stimulated by the new challenge, and after the defeat at Alarcos, the military orders still formed a stout barrier across the central tablelands. Eventually, the storm broke. At last learning the folly of their ways, the Christian kingdoms decided to unite forces and make a combined attack on the Moslem south. On July 16, 1212, at Las Navas de Tolosa, they won the decisive battle of the Reconquest, the battle that was to open up to them the south itself.

The disintegration once more into separate states of Moslem authority in al-Andalus facilitated the Christian advance, not least because the rival powers sought Christian aid against one another. In 1236, Ferdinand III of Castile and León captured the ancient capital, Córdoba itself, almost without a struggle. In 1238 Valencia and the Balearic Islands fell; in 1246 Jaén, and in 1248 Seville, capitulated. Only one *taifa* kingdom remained. At the siege of Jaén, the ruler of Granada had approached Saint Ferdinand, undertaken to pay tribute, and offered his collaboration in the siege of Seville. These terms accepted, the kingdom of Granada acquired a form of autonomy under the Nasrid dynasty which kept it inviolate until the end of the fifteenth century. Stretching from Almería to Gibraltar, from Granada to the south coast, this area remained for 250 years the only surviving fragment of al-Andalus, at once a monument to that ambiguity which had already characterized relations between north and south and an anachronism in a Peninsula that was now officially Christian. The Alhambra, exquisite palace of the Nasrid kings, survives to this day as a symbol of the vanished glories of Spanish Islam.

The military Reconquest, once it gathered direction and momentum, had been swiftly accomplished. The long centuries of slow territorial erosion had given way, once the will to reclaim the whole of the

Peninsula had crystallized, to a short period of concerted military
attacks which had engulfed most of Moslem Spain in the space of a
mere thirty-six years. But if the Moslem regime had ended, everywhere
save Granada, the Moslems themselves, the Spaniards who worshiped
Allah, remained. Like the Jews, they constituted a problem that would
somehow have to be solved. Similarly, conquering the south was not
enough; it had to be Christianized, colonized, and repopulated. These
problems belong more properly to the history of Christian Spain, so
suffice it to say at the moment that this Reconquest too was achieved,
though what it produced was a complex and many-layered society
whose lack of homogeneity became increasingly manifest as the years
passed. It was during these centuries that Spain came really face to face
with problems created by the division of the Peninsula into a Christian
north and a Moslem south. While the two had remained strong and
separate, coexistence of a sort had proved feasible, but the political
demise of the one gave rise to social, racial, and religious complexities
which the other ultimately found it impossible to absorb. The Spanish
Moslems, great assimilators and adaptors that they were, had done
nothing but good to their Spain, commercially, industrially, agricul-
turally, and culturally. They had created a brilliant civilization at a
time when the rulers of the north were little more than tribal chieftains.
They had possessed a country which, because of them, was for a time
the envy of all Europe. Yet their political identity gone, they soon
found themselves a despised and subject people, so despised and so
subject that like the Spanish Jews they were eventually forced to leave
their homeland altogether. All they had had to give, to teach, to pass
on, was taken, but they themselves were rejected. The double-thinking
so characteristic of the human mind led to a romanticization of the
defeated Moslem knight in the Spanish literature of the fifteenth and
sixteenth centuries, but the contradiction is more apparent than real.
For the fiction of the "sentimental Moor" and the reality of the Moslem
laborer living in his ghetto outside the city walls, are essentially the
same: both present the former citizen of the proud state of al-Andalus
as an emasculated figure.

C un pintor pintaua a omagen de S̃ꝗ. mꝛ fremosa ꞇ a o dͤmo muy.

C o dͤmo pꝛceu a o pintor ꞇ meteo muy mal p ꝗ o pintaua feo.

C o pintor pintaua hũa omagen d̃ ... S̃ꝗ ꞇ ꞇ ꝗna vꝺa touaꝛ ...

C o dͤmo ꝺalgũ o Gaudio ... viuor uel ficou colgaꝺo ...

C agẽte ueo ao ruꝺo ꞇ uiu̅ h̃ ... gꝛ o dͤmo ꞇ o pintor estaꝺ ...

C tota agẽte deu lo̅ a S̃ꝗ. ꞇ este miragꝛ ꝗ fe ...

CHAPTER III

THE CHRISTIAN ASCENDANCY

The moment has now come to review the centuries of Moslem presence on Spanish soil from the standpoint of the Christian north, to trace the emergence and slow, difficult rise to supremacy of the powers which were to effect the re-entry of the Peninsula into European Christendom. The traditional picture of a "Moorish" Occupation and a Christian Reconquest has already been seen to be a vastly oversimplified one. The impression too often given is that of a massive invasion of Moorish hordes who drove the Christian natives from their homelands into the mountain fastnesses of the far north, from which vantage point the dispatriated Spaniards waged a long, heroic war of reconquest, gradually pushing the invaders back and reclaiming the country for Spain and for Christianity. But such an impression is valid only at a superficial military level.

The two Spains were never thus clearly divided; they overlapped and, particularly in the south, overlay each other. The majority of the inhabitants remained in their homes in occupied territory and large numbers of them became apostates. As for the resistance that sprang up in the far north, this originated in regions which at first harried the

A medieval mural painter is miraculously saved from death by the Holy Virgin, in an illustration from a late thirteenth-century manuscript.

Moslems, not so much from any sense of national or religious purpose, as out of a general sense of hostility toward the foreigner and a desire for land. Even as the territorial imperative grew, it manifested itself in aggression almost as much against other Christian groupings as against the Moslems themselves. Not for many centuries was this crucial hindrance to the fortunes of Christian Spain overcome by a full awareness of what unity could achieve in the name of national consciousness and religious crusade. The mood of the Christians of the north was not so heroic that local interests could easily be sacrificed to higher issues.

The fact remains, however, that it was to one of these regions, Asturias, that the remnants of King Roderick's army, court, and administration fled. They were able to some extent to control and direct the natural ferocity of the people of the mountains. More important, these Visigoths and their descendants do seem to have kept alive some notion of a political destiny, of a legitimate claim to power inherited through them by Asturias from the former Visigothic monarchy. It was a concept that had more substance in princely imagination and scribes' records than in political reality, and probably no substance at all in the popular consciousness. But it was a concept that somehow survived and which destiny was eventually to clothe in the flesh of reality. It would be wrong, however, to take this Asturian claim to legitimacy as being anything more tangible in the early centuries, as the flame from which grew the raging fire of a reconquest. This is obvious from the events that took place, slightly later, to the east, in the foothills of the Pyrenees. Like the Cantabrians, the mountaineers here too began to push south out of a general sense of antagonism and a desire for more land to pasture their flocks. As time rewarded their efforts, their movement into Islamic territory constituted a reconquest of their own, parallel with, yet separate from, that traced by the Christian peoples farther west.

Neither history nor legend tells us much about these early efforts of the people of the Pyrenees, but with the Asturian victory at Covadonga in 718, they made their mark upon both. In spite of the spectacular legend that four hundred thousand Moslems were killed when all the weapons thrown by the infidel miraculously flew back at them, the far less dramatic truth is simply that the Asturians under their leader Pelayo, the first hero of the Reconquest, defeated a small force of marauding Moslems in a skirmish. Pelayo's real achievement was in fact more considerable. He carved out a tiny kingdom for himself there in the wild north and then set Asturias the task of re-establishing that political authority which in the midst of all the other Visigothic splendors had crumbled into dust before the onslaught of Islam. The tiny nugget of the Christian monarchy founded by Pelayo painfully grew under the rule of able successors until, by the end of the eighth century, Asturias extended its sway from the province of Galicia in the west to Santander in the east, with its capital at Oviedo. The first steps on the long road back to a Christian Spain had been taken.

Although not an encounter of any military importance, the Battle of Covadonga did have the effect of dissuading the enemy from encroaching upon territory it was not much interested in anyway. The Moslems continued to raid well up into the north but were content to settle farther south in the sun. When they withdrew each time across the plateau they laid waste the land behind, creating the vast no man's land which came to separate the two societies and which so seriously impeded the Christian advance. For just as the Moslems were too few to secure their hold on so vast an expanse of territory as the Peninsula, so the Christian north likewise lacked the human resources to defend properly the land they won. And when that land was devastated, persuading people to leave their homes and to recolonize this barren frontier territory became a problem of gigantic proportions. It was a problem that rendered people a more desirable form of booty than gold and the fact that they were being reclaimed for Christianity was only an added incentive. It was a problem that has led historians to regard the Christian repopulation of Spain as the true Reconquest.

It was a problem, furthermore, which accounts for certain important features of subsequent Spanish life. Herding animals was an easier way at once of absorbing territory and of protecting one's livelihood in times of danger than tilling the soil, and this confirmed the existing tendency toward a pastoral rather than an agricultural economy in the Christian kingdoms. Politically, the difficulties resulted in the granting of municipal privileges that became a feature of medieval Spanish society. On ground won from the Moslems, old towns were repopulated with Christians and new towns established through the encouragement of grants of *fueros,* individual charters, offered to any prepared to go and live in them. Serfs from the north who found their way to such towns became free citizens, and some of the early *fueros* were explicitly applicable to Jews and Moslems as well. These *fueros* became possessions which towns and villages clung to proudly and determinedly throughout the centuries of turbulence that formed the Middle Ages. They created legal confusion, but at the same time they were an effective impediment to the establishment of a rule of might, and produced independent communities which played a significant role in the protracted battle between Crown and nobility. They encouraged, in fact, a spirit of independence which would lead to popular representation in Spain more than a hundred years earlier than in England —in Aragon in 1133, in Castile in 1169.

The Christians soon found that holding the ground they had won proved more difficult than the initial act of winning it. And they often lost what had been gained at considerable cost only a short time before. Nevertheless, they gradually extended the territory which could be regarded as permanently reclaimed. Their progress was as confused as it was slow. Alliances were not tidily based on religious faith or

on hostility to the Moslems—as the Battle of Roncesvalles will serve to remind us: to the north of the Pyrenees the Franks had blocked the Arab advance and then helped resettle Hispanic exiles on the lands to the immediate south of the great mountain barrier. But when Charlemagne marched to the relief of Saragossa in 778, it was not so much with the aim of pushing back the Moslem frontier for Christianity as of striking a blow against Abd-al-Rahman I on behalf of the caliph of Baghdad. And when the expedition ended in defeat at the hands of

The brave Roland sounds a horn to alert his warriors to approaching danger.

the unexpectedly hostile citizens of Saragossa, Charlemagne's army, robbed of their rightful spoils, sacked instead Pamplona, the center of the Christian kingdom of Navarre. As a result, when the Franks retreated through the Pyrenees, their rear guard was attacked in the famous Roncesvalles Pass, not by Moslem troops as the *Chanson de Roland* claims, though some may have participated, but by Basques incensed by the destruction of their capital. Roland and many of his peers died not for their faith but as retribution for a sordid piece of military misbehavior. Perhaps as a result of this episode, Spanish suspicion of their northern neighbors, who were logically their natural allies, overcame religious differences at home to the extent that when Alfonso II of Asturias appealed to Charlemagne for aid in extending his boundaries, his nobles forced him to withdraw from the alliance.

If Frankish influence and help was firmly rejected in the central north, the Franks fared better on the eastern seaboard. After their rout at Saragossa, they embarked upon the conquest of Catalonia. And while Navarre to the west established its independence as a monarchy in the middle of the ninth century, the Catalan counties that sprang into being during the course of Charlemagne's campaigns were incorporated into the Carolingian Empire as an amorphous political body known as the Spanish March. Its connection with the empire was close and although an independent dynasty of counts was later established with Guifré the Hairy, the flavor of life in the March was essentially French rather than Iberian. A rigorous feudal system was developed on the pattern that was taking shape in Europe as a whole and from which the rest of Spain remained apart owing to the peculiar circumstances of its growth. Catalonia was closer to the rest of Europe and closer to Rome, and culturally as well as socially she looked north instead of west or south. As a result, she has always remained one of the main avenues through which cultural influences in general have entered Spain from the outside. Not without some cause have the Catalans been called the Europeans of Spain.

For all the xenophobia of the Christian north, a dramatic event in the reign of Alfonso II (791–842) brought France and Europe into the Peninsula. At the same time it was, paradoxically, the first milestone in the rise of Spanish Christian nationalism. This was the miraculous discovery, by a star-guided shepherd in a Galician field, of the

Olite Castle, the palace of the kings of Navarre until the fifteenth century

remains of James the Apostle, who according to legend had preached the gospel in Spain. At one stroke Spain acquired a patron saint and Europe one of its foremost places of pilgrimage. Thenceforth, Saint James the Moor-killer, or Santiago Mata-moros, was seen always to lead the Christians into battle and his name became their war cry: *Santiago y cierre España!* (Saint James and charge, Spain!)

Near the site of the miracle grew up the city of Santiago de Compostela (field of the star) with a church to house the holy relic. This structure, which was later destroyed by fire, was replaced in the eleventh and twelfth centuries by the glorious Romanesque cathedral that survives today. Here, displaying the cockleshells that distinguished them as pilgrims of Santiago, flocked the penitent of Europe, Chaucer's Wife of Bath among them. Over the years the pilgrim way from the Pyrenees, or the French Road as it came to be called, became a channel through which cultural influences from the outside world entered Spain. Churches and monasteries showing the influence of the latest developments in European architecture sprang up along the way—the great Romanesque cathedral at Jaca is a splendid example of the civilizing results of these outside contacts. The Road became, too, an eloquent geographical pointer to the fortunes of the Christian kingdoms. For as the Christian rulers forced back the perimeter of securely held territory, the pilgrims understandably abandoned the hazards of a journey through mountainous Asturias in favor of the gentler, more southerly routes, until by the end of the eleventh century they were passing through the very heart of Old Castile, Burgos itself.

In the meantime, the Christian north was gradually taking shape. In 987 the Spanish March achieved autonomy from the Frankish Empire. The region that thanks to the Franks had experienced only one hundred years of Moslem rule now set off on its own road through history. To the west as we have seen, Navarre had already thrown off Frankish imperial ties. Still farther to the west, Asturias by the beginning of the tenth century had grown into a kingdom that stretched westward to include Galicia and southward to envelop León. Galicia in its turn had stretched some way down into what had once been the Roman province of Lusitania. The pattern of the Reconquest from now on becomes one of vertical expansion downward from these northern starting points in center, east, and west.

A sixteenth-century painting by Juan de Flandres shows Santiago, patron saint
of Spain, triumphing in a fierce battle with the hated infidels.

Until the fall of the caliphate in 1012, progress south was painfully slow and—because the Christians were only able to retain the land they had won by accepting vassalage to al-Andalus—highly unsatisfactory. Their inability to consolidate their successes was in large part due to their primitive view of the meaning of kingship. For them a kingdom was a personal estate that belonged to the king to divide up as he wished among his various sons. This disastrous interpretation led to the repeated disintegration of a power structure that had been built up by years of blood and toil. Obviously intended to quell sibling rivalry, these divisions succeeded only in encouraging fratricidal strife as the heirs fought for repossession of the whole. The kingdom of Asturias first disintegrated, in fact, as the result of a situation in which the heirs could not even wait for their father's death before enforcing this system of inheritance. The kingdom was divided into three: Asturias proper, Galicia, and León. Soon after, León and Galicia merged and the capital was transferred to the city of León itself. The kaleidoscopic movement of the Christian kingdoms—separating, merging again, and forever forming different power patterns—is a peculiar feature of the Spanish Middle Ages and with the complication of al-Andalus makes Spain's medieval history the most complex and confused in Europe. But the merger of Galicia and León is a landmark in that León, larger and nearer the arena of action than the little mountain kingdom in the north, succeeded Asturias as the center of gravity.

The shift in the balance of power brought León into direct contact with the caliphate of Córdoba. Abd-al-Rahman III, the first caliph, had ably reorganized the military and political affairs of al-Andalus, but his efforts came just too late. He was able to push back the armies of León and Navarre but not as far as the mountain valleys from which they had emerged. The Christians had gained a viable foothold on the central plateau. And they had no intention of giving it up.

The military superiority of the caliphate brought home to the kings of León the need to consolidate their gains if they were not to lose them. As a first step they introduced the policy of repopulation by reward. Extensive privileges attracted the hardy, the needy, and the bold to the old and new settlements of the Duero tableland. And their survival on this majestic but arid plateau was protected by a series of castles or fortified towns. These became so familiar a sight on the

austere, war-ravaged landscape and so characteristic of the region,
that this part of the kingdom of León came to be known by the name
of Castile. Castile's geographical position in relation to the retreating
enemy soon cast her in the spearhead role hitherto occupied by León.
Asturias had spawned León and León had spawned Castile and in each
case the offspring had usurped the parent's position.

The contrast between Castile, which achieved the status of a semi-
autonomous county within the Leonese monarchy, and the mother
kingdom very quickly became marked. While León found inspiration
in the past, Castile, rawly new and unfettered by traditions or nostalgia,
had her eyes fixed firmly on the future. The city of León itself had been
a Roman settlement, whereas Burgos, one of the fortified *villas* that
gave Castile its name, was hardly more than a few decades old. León
ruled itself on the basis of the *Liber Judiciorum,* while Castile met
the new problems of a territory forged by war by making its own
laws as it went along. Even linguistically Castile assumed the lead. It
was populated by migrations of mountaineers from the far north whose
tongue was more emphatic and more primitive than the romance
language spoken across the greater part of the Christian north. As
Castile took the forefront of activities the language became transformed from a backwater dialect into a vigorous innovatory vernacular
to form the Castilian that became modern Spanish.

A region of such obvious dynamism was not likely to remain for long
subject to León, and as Leonese nobles fought the Crown out of personal ambition and regional pride, Castilian autonomy gradually became a reality. It was a struggle in which the caliphate itself was
intimately involved, illustrating once again the ambiguity of relations
between north and south. This is another of those points in the growth
of Spain where history and legend meet and, like all such points, the
moment has its epic hero. Fernán González, who died in 970 and was
subsequently immortalized in chronicles, ballads, and the thirteenth-
century *Poema de Fernán González,* was the first to assume the formal
title of Count of Castile. Legend ascribes the independence of Castile
to his appearance one day before the king of León with a horse and a
hawk so beautiful that the king insisted on buying them and promised
to double the price for every day that payment was delayed. After
many years had gone by and the money had still not been paid, the sum

involved was so prohibitive that only the independence of his county could repay the count.

Sadly, history paints a more prosaic picture. Fernán González, after winning notable successes against the Moslems both for himself and for León, came out in open rebellion against his king, Ramiro II (*r.* 930–950). González repeatedly joined the Moslems in their expeditions against León and all attempts to deprive him of authority proved so futile that the Leonese king, now Sancho the Fat, was driven in desperation to seek the help of the caliph against him. Unfortunately, Sancho's political reliance on the Moslems was less successful than his private appeal to the caliph's doctors to cure his obesity. Moslem medicine reduced his weight, but Moslem military backing proved less effective in controlling the ambitions of the count. Dynastic rivalry within León, into which both Fernán González and the kingdom of Navarre poked powerful interfering fingers, eventually enabled the count to establish Castile's independence. And his standing among his own nobles and subjects was such that he was able to achieve something that the Asturo-Leonese monarchs, for all their claim to legitimacy, had proved incapable of doing—investing the succession of authority firmly in his own heirs.

Castile's status changed from county to that of kingdom in the eleventh century, as the result of the murder of the last Castilian count, a young boy, on the eve of his wedding day. Sancho the Great of Navarre (*r.* 1000–1035) inherited Castile through his wife, the young count's elder sister. At his death, he divided his extensive domain among four sons, bequeathing Castile to Ferdinand, his second son. (Navarre went to his firstborn; the county of Aragon to another; the lesser remaining lands to the last.) Two years later Ferdinand assumed the title of King of Castile, and in the same year, 1037, he reestablished Castile's old ties by defeating the king of León and Galicia in a pitched battle. The once subject county had emerged as the dominant state in the Christian north. In the meantime territorial gains on the part of his brother brought Aragon into contact with Catalonia in the east and with Moslem Saragossa in the south. These were to prove the two main areas of Aragonese activities—political and commercial on the one hand, military and expansionist on the other—in the years to come. Aragon too would grow from a county into a kingdom.

An illustration of medieval music making from the Cantigas, *a thirteenth-century manuscript of songs compiled by Alfonso X, king of León and Castile*

To Sancho the Great, therefore, must go the responsibility for indirectly deciding the future pattern of medieval Spain. Being half-Castilian himself and having been brought up in Castile, it seems appropriate that he should have fathered Castile's elevation to national status. Sancho's importance, however, is not limited to the role he played in the creation of Spain's two great kingdoms. Navarre straddled the Pyrenees to include the Basques on both sides, and in consequence her destiny for centuries to come was to be closely linked with that of France. Inevitably, she became a channel of European influence into the western Peninsula, reinforcing that provided by the French Road. And Sancho himself made one significant contribution to this cultural connection. In 1024 he formally admitted into Spain the reformed Order of Cluny which had entered the Peninsula shortly before at the Catalan monastery of Ripoll. The Hispanic liturgy had been virtually arrested at that point in time when the Peninsula had been severed from Europe by the Moslem invasion, and it was now very different from that of Rome. The script used in Spanish monasteries was still the Visigothic uncial script, and the Christian Church in León had become a national body subject to the Crown only. The Cluniac reform, on the other hand, sought to tighten the bonds between religious life and Rome. Naturally this meant that Sancho's momentous decision did not go unopposed. But although the Roman reforms were not fully implemented in León until the reign of Sancho's grandson, the Order made itself felt much earlier and in a crucial way: at the instigation of Cluniac monks the pope, in 1063, named the Peninsula as an area of holy crusade. The Reconquest had become a European concern.

Castile was by now firmly established in its position at the forefront of Peninsula politics. A new society which had emerged from an old one, it had all the qualities necessary to maintain its position. The Leonese inheritance—a craft industry, a flourishing monastic life, a chancellery—gave the new kingdom solidity and depth, while the war-reared peasants and shepherds, who were the mass of its people, imparted an air of virility and democracy that became its hallmark. It was for centuries a revolutionary society after the manner of all pioneer societies. Concerned with the present, it rejected the Visigothic past from its earliest days—Count García Fernández, Fernán González' son, for example, doubled the number of Castilian knights from about 250 to 500, raising to the rank of lesser nobility, or *infan-zonía,* any man who could go to war on his own horse. Castile was born to war and suckled on war, and it was in war, as historian Jaime Vicéns Vives said, that she "forged her warrior temperament, her will to command, and her ambition to achieve a great destiny."

With the downfall of the caliphate, Castile was not slow to make good the opportunity. Its rulers set about the reduction of the Moslem *reinos de taifa* to the rank of tributaries of Castile, and its sway was extended from the Mediterranean to the Atlantic. Ferdinand I of Castile himself envassaled Toledo, Seville, and Badajoz. Yet unbelievably, this monarch too, who had spent close to twenty years consolidating his position in the north, was persuaded before his death in 1065 to share among his three sons the realm he had painfully pieced together. Divided once more into Castile, León, and Galicia, with the kingdoms and counties to the east completing a disintegration that matched that of the Moslem south, the inheritance fell prey yet again to civil strife. Sancho II (*r.* 1065–1072), insatiable inheritor of Castile, declared war in turn upon his brothers in Navarre, León, and Galicia and even laid siege to his sister Urraca's portion, Zamora. His assassination one dark night in 1077 before Zamora—an event that has become the stuff of literature and legend and out of which Sancho has somehow emerged as a sympathetic figure—led to the reuniting of Castile with León under his exiled brother Alfonso VI (*r.* 1072–1109).

The confusing labyrinth of Spanish medieval history tends to reduce its numerous monarchs to an anonymous cavalcade of ghostly disembodied crowns. Those kings that have survived the deadening effects of sheer numbers in the public memory and popular history have done so for varied and often eccentric reasons: Sancho the Fat because of his name, Sancho the Great because of his last will and testament that indirectly created the kingdom of Castile and Aragon. Alfonso VI now owes his fame to his connection with Ruy Díaz de Bivar, otherwise known by his Arabic title as El Cid, the *infanzón* who emerged from the small village near Burgos where he was born, to become the governor of Valencia and the very embodiment of Castile's national destiny for all posterity. The hero of Spain's earliest surviving epic poem—a splendid work of very great qualities written in the late twelfth or early thirteenth century, called the *Cantar de mío Cid*—and of ballad,

stage, and lately screen, El Cid was inevitably a less perfect figure than tradition has painted him and his traditional identity may even be an amalgam of two individuals. In the *Cantar* he is a grave, majestic figure who can subdue lions at a glance and who wears his beard in a net to avoid the dishonor of having it tweaked. He stands for personal dignity and integrity, for social justice and the rule of law, even for racial and religious tolerance. Exiled by his young king, he reacts impeccably and eventually succeeds in teaching him true kingliness. In life, El Cid's relations with his king do seem to have been strained—possibly because he is thought to have taken a leading role in the dramatic episode in which Alfonso was made to swear by the Bible that he had no hand in his brother Sancho's death—and during his period of exile from Castile he fought against Christians under the banner of the Moslem ruler of Saragossa. El Cid's basic loyalties, however, were to Castile and Alfonso. He played a noteworthy part in Castile's offensive against Span-

Ramón Berenguer, eleventh-century count of Barcelona, spearing a Moor

ish Islam and in 1094 conquered Valencia in Alfonso's name. On his death in 1099 his wife Jimena held Valencia for three years until it fell to the Almoravides. Of the fair and famous Jimena we are told very little in the *Cantar,* for it is a poem written about men in an age of men. But her presence is captured in a single line describing the occasion when El Cid proudly takes his wife and daughters onto the battlements at Valencia to survey the recently conquered Moslem town at their feet—"Beautiful eyes gaze all around." Our imagination does the rest.

Alfonso VI does not really deserve to be overshadowed by a figure of dubious historical accuracy, however splendid. Whatever his responsibility for his brother's assassination might have been, he was an able monarch who made his reign a memorable one. He raided southward as far as Córdoba and Seville and in 1082 even reached the Mediterranean at Tarifa. But the great, lasting achievement came in 1085, when with the aid of foreign crusaders he captured the former Visigothic capital of Toledo. An event of tremendous symbolic significance for the whole of a rejoicing Europe, the victory was also strategically a big step forward. It brought the Christians down from the wastelands in the north into the heart of Spain and made possible the secure repopulation of the intervening territory. New Castile and the cities of Madrid, Alcalá de Henares, Segovia, and Ávila came into being, and the Christians now looked down on the pulse of Islamic Spain, the rich, fertile plains of Andalusia. With most of the *taifa* states in tribute to the north, supremacy seemed to be in sight and Alfonso accordingly assumed the title of "king of the two religions." This state of mind was, however, soon to end.

The change, as we saw earlier, was precipitated by the arrival from Africa in 1086 of the Almoravides. Their intransigence and the victories it brought them not unnaturally evoked a corresponding religious hostility among their opponents. The ideal of a full-scale crusade, of a Christian Reconquest, began to crystallize. Those Moslems whose deep roots in Spanish soil gave them every right to consider themselves Spaniards came to be regarded as alien intruders, a living insult to the pride of a Spain that had once been united in Christianity. The ideal of purification, of an elimination from the body of Spain of all elements considered spiritually noxious, began to take hold of the Spanish Christian conscience, and Spain tentatively assumed the religious destiny that was profoundly to influence her path through the centuries.

The crusading spirit was not yet so entrenched, however, as to galvanize the north into concerted military action. Neither was it sufficiently formulated to allow the Castilians to handle easily the problem presented by the mass of Moslems and Jews who had been incorporated wholesale into Castile with Alfonso's acquisition of their territory. They represented the craftsmen, merchants, and agricultural workers whom the Christians could ill afford to lose. They stayed therefore, a thorn in the side of Christian Spain which was to fester and grow as more and more land was conquered, until such time as it would be ruthlessly—and disastrously—wrenched out.

The geographical and political face of Christian Spain, in the meantime, continued to change. On the marriage of Alfonso's daughter, Teresa, to Henry of Burgundy, they received as dowry the land to the south of Galicia, the county of Portugal. Castile itself was shortly torn by internal disorder. Alfonso VI had engaged the support of his nobles in his southern campaigns by granting them large tracts of reconquered territory. The policy had also served as the best means of maintaining the new frontiers, which could not have been adequately protected by the Crown itself. With land, however, came power, and as the power of the nobles grew, their position vis-à-vis the monarchy became stronger and their demands increased, creating a permanent tension between the monarchy and aristocracy which was paralleled in nearly every other country in western Europe in the Middle Ages; in Spain it would explode into civil war in the fifteenth century. This dissension in Castile allowed Portuguese ambition to flower, and in 1143 Teresa's son proclaimed his independence from Castile. Unlike that of all the other medieval kingdoms and counties of the Peninsula, the independence of Portugal was to remain a political reality. Only for a period of sixty years, four and a half centuries later, was Portugal ever again subject to the fulcrum of Peninsular power in the center.

Castile's dreams of Peninsular unity under an imperial title, seated of course in Castile itself, received a severe blow from Portugal's declaration of independence. But the movement away from integration was not solely a western one. In the east too the pattern of future development was emerging. Castilian attempts at empire building, such as the occupation of Saragossa, inevitably led Aragon to seek support from Catalonia in the east. Ramiro II of Aragon—Ramiro the Monk as he is known—took the crucial step of marrying his daughter to Ramón Berenguer IV, the count of Barcelona, and then in 1137 retiring to a monastery, leaving the government of his kingdom in the hands of his eminently capable son-in-law. The partnership of the kingdom of Aragon and the principality of Catalonia that with Valencia and the Balearics later on was to constitute the Crown of Aragon was thus born.

The significance of this step for Aragon was enormous. It meant that she turned her back on Castile, and with Catalonia faced eastward into the Mediterranean and northward to France. Furthermore it was a partnership taken without loss of autonomy or individuality on either side. Aragon by virtue of its monarchy remained the seat of titular authority with its capital at Saragossa, Catalonia becoming the vital cosmopolitan, commercial pulse of the Crown. They coexisted in harmony and unity of purpose without either falling prey to the other—a political solution to the Peninsula's separatist tendencies with which Castile unfortunately was never able to come to terms. Together the Aragonese and Catalans were able to push the Moslems out of southern Catalonia; trade with the Mediterranean expanded and flourished; and through Catalonia Aragon was exposed to the refining influences of France's cultural center in Provence and Languedoc. To Catalonia Aragon brought political authority within the Peninsula; to Aragon Catalonia brought new and wider horizons far beyond it.

The two sovereignties made a formidable team with which Castile was forced to reckon. Treaties were signed which mapped out clearly defined and separate zones of Moslem territory for reconquest by the two powers. The clarification thus achieved allowed the Christian kingdoms to pursue their territorial aims relatively undisturbed. It also made concerted efforts against the enemy a more acceptable solution to the Christian offensive than hitherto in that the outcome in case of victory was less fraught with ambiguity.

In the twelfth century the pace of reconquest quickened. Granada and Seville were sacked, the south coast was reached, Córdoba was won and then lost again. The Almoravid and Almohad invasions in the short term slowed the advance but in the long run contributed to it. The creation of the military orders, formed in direct response to the invasions, made an indelible mark on the physical and spiritual face of the north. Forming as the orders did the permanent front line of both defense and attack, the territorial rewards for their efforts were commensurately great. The ethos they represented and fostered was one of harsh intransigence. Created specifically as crusading organs, their material well-being could only be enhanced by the stimulation, through religious and racial prejudice, of the need to conquer and repossess, and it is significant that the lands they controlled more than any other region fostered the spirit of aggression and intolerance toward the Moslems which came to characterize the Reconquest.

Castile at this crucial moment in its development was particularly blessed with able, energetic monarchs. Alfonso VII (*r.* 1126–1157), the son of El Cid's King Alfonso, was one of these. His imperial vision had carried Castilian troops into Saragossa and his conquering zeal had driven them to the south coast. He persuaded the pope to elevate the diocese of Santiago into an archbishopric and made Toledo a European center for scholarly and literary activities that were mainly devoted to the translation of Hebrew, Arabic, and Greek works. Castile was beginning to make its mark upon the face of European culture and civilization. Even Alfonso, however, as he approached death, was reduced to imitating the cautious family niceties of his predecessors. By leaving Castile and León to different sons he condemned the kingdoms to almost half a century of intermittent civil war. The disastrous effects of his will culminated in the crushing defeat suffered by the Christians at Alarcos in 1195 when Castile was abandoned at the very last moment by fickle León and Navarre.

The kingdom of León repeated the betrayal at the Battle of Las Navas de Tolosa seventeen years later. But this time Castile had the help of other kingdoms and foreign crusaders. In June, 1212 (a year as famous in Spanish history as 1066 is in English history), knights and men-at-arms from across the north of Spain congregated in Toledo with crusaders from all over Europe. Once assembled they marched south, their aim to strike at the very heart of Andalusia. Shepherds guided them along the sheep and goat tracks that served as passes through the wild Sierra Morena—the mountain barrier that cuts off the lush south from the arid wastes of the central plateau. Daunted by the difficulties and by the cold, many of the foreign crusaders turned

back, but the home armies, hardened by the rigors of the Spanish
climate and terrain, pressed on until they poured out of the Sierra onto
the great rolling plain of Tolosa. The Moslems, who could so easily
have ambushed the Christian forces in the mountains, had made the
gigantic tactical error of awaiting their arrival. In the clash that followed, the Christians won the decisive battle of the Reconquest.

Las Navas de Tolosa marks the great turning point. The African
impetus was spent and no remedy was forthcoming for the renewed
discord inside al-Andalus. The Christian kingdoms now moved south
more or less in unison. Most important, the advantage gained at Las
Navas was driven home by Castile's next king, the great Ferdinand III
(r. 1217–1252). He dominates a century of Christian victories, and his
dedication to the furthering of the Christian cause led after his death
to his canonization as Saint Ferdinand. After the collapse of Almohad
power, the rich trophies of Islamic Spain fell like ninepins before the
northern armies. Portugal's armies reached the southern coast first,
but Castile won the greatest prize, Andalusia. In the east Valencia fell
before the Catalan-Aragonese offensive. But as the troops of the Crown
of Aragon continued south, Ferdinand, who was as wily as he was
zealous, managed to slip in and make the Moslem kingdom of Murcia
—a logical extension for Aragonese sovereignty—a Castilian possession. Castile was able to bring off this ambitious move partly because
her authority and military strength had been enormously increased
by union with the mother kingdom, León. (Ferdinand, heir to the
Leonese throne but son of a Castilian mother, by a quirk of fate had
succeeded to both crowns.) And this time the two kingdoms were reunited for good. The processes of human mortality and natural selec-
tion had resolved the love-hate relationship in the figure of a man
farsighted enough to ensure by the terms of his own will that Castile
and León should never more be divided.

Ferdinand III was both the embodiment of the thirteenth-century
crusading spirit and to a very large extent the impetus behind it. An
inspired leader and gifted strategist, he made sure that his successes
were marked by events of material and symbolic importance. He recon-
secrated the great mosque at Córdoba as a cathedral and sent captured
Moslems to Santiago with the cathedral bells which al-Mansur had
carried off over two centuries before. More practically, he celebrated

the fall of Seville by immediately building shipyards there and laying the foundations for a Castilian fleet. Castile's great maritime future was born at this point. When Ferdinand died in 1252, the Reconquest effectively died too, not to be revived for another two centuries. The Christians had, for the time being, run out of crusading breath.

The exhaustion was not surprising. Within the space of one generation Andalusia, Valencia, and the Balearics had all been wrested from the Moslems' grip and resettled. Repopulation meant that the butter of Spanish Christendom's human resources was now more thinly spread over a much vaster area of bread. Furthermore, resettlement in itself was at all levels a time- and energy-absorbing task. It was a task carried out on completely different organizational bases by the Crowns of Castile and Aragon. Andalusia was virtually divided by Saint Ferdinand among the nobles who had helped him in the Reconquest, thus its large-estate system, little changed since Roman days, survived the great territorial upheaval. At one stroke Ferdinand made the south an aristocrat- and peasant-based community quite distinct from the more democratic north with its bourgeoisie and its strong municipalities; and by doing so he vastly increased the power of his nobles. In the absence of the independent small holder, the economy of Andalusia acquired a pastoral orientation which was destined to meet the growing needs of the northern European and Italian wool trade and bring quick profits. Valencia, on the other hand, which remained a kingdom within the multiple Crown of Aragon, was resettled largely by Catalan farmers and knights and only in a very limited way by Aragonese barons. Valencia's richly cultivated land therefore did not suffer in the way that Andalusia's did from the change of ownership, and the orchards so lovingly cultivated by the Moslems continued to flourish. That the Moslems themselves—"Mudejars" now, under Christian rule —were happy to stay on in Valencia and continue their orchard husbandry, ensured the continuation of a prosperous economy; and a flourishing Catalan merchant fleet carried their produce and that of Moslem artisans to a wide European market. In Andalusia the agrarian situation, already suffering from the lack of a native merchant fleet, reached a crisis pitch with the expulsion of the Mudejar peasants in 1263 after a Moslem rebellion.

The expulsion of the Mudejars is another milestone in the social

Anti-Semitism is evident in this manuscript illustration of Jews illicitly obtaining and then abusing the Eucharist.

history of the Peninsula. The three religious communities of Spain had managed to coexist in commendable harmony under the Moslems and during the early centuries of the Reconquest. North and south had tolerated minorities, political and military considerations had overcome sectarian differences, and commercial and cultural relations were so close as to blur both racial and religious distinctions. Even after Berber fanaticism had introduced the harsh note of official religious discrimination and oppression, the three communities continued to live side by side in a comparatively open society. New Castile—the major area of mixed population before the south was conquered—adopted the tri-communal system of coexistence, whereby Moslems, Christians, and Jews lived peaceably together in different quarters in each town. A common intellectual life continued under the Christians to be the vital reality it had been under Moslem rule, revealing a refreshing ability to survive the adverse changes in the social and political climate.

Although Saint Ferdinand was happy to proclaim himself "king of the three religions," Christian supremacy when it came made religious tolerance a dispensable commodity. Aggression against "the infidel" had become for the north, particularly for Castile, a way of thinking and a way of life, and it was not suddenly to be dissipated with military victory. On the contrary, victory confirmed the conquerors' sense of superiority. Furthermore, it disrupted the traditional division of roles of Spain's multiracial society in New Castile, where the Christian had been warrior and peasant, the Moslem cultivator and artisan, and the Jew technician and trader. Officially, religious toleration, in the sense of there being no policy of forced conversion, continued. The anti-Jewish legislation of the Council of Arles in 1235, which ordered all Jews to wear over their hearts a yellow disc of identification, was not enforced in Spain in the thirteenth century, and the Inquisition established in Aragon in 1238 was concerned only with Christian heretics, and anyway gradually declined into inactivity.

While the Jewish population to some extent occupied a privileged position due to their financial role in the Christian economy, the Moslems of the south were soon reduced to the status of servants in their own homes. Like the Mudejars incorporated earlier on into Christian society farther north, they were used as rural laborers, artisans, and carriers. In the towns they had formerly owned they became under-

privileged, merely tolerated, inferior beings who were usually compelled to dwell outside the city walls. Little wonder then that they
should look with longing toward the Moslem kingdom of Granada and
even with a faint hope toward the shores of their religious brethren in
North Africa. The revolt of the Moslem peasants of Andalusia and
Murcia in collusion with Granada in 1263 confirmed the Christians'
growing fears of fifth-column activities on the part of their Moslem
subjects and led to the expulsion of large numbers of them. The precedent for solving the problem of religious nonconformity by the drastic
expedient of expulsion had been set. Castile's sensitivity to the close
presence of religious dissidents in fact continued to determine the
channels into which she directed her energies even after the completion
of the major state of the Reconquest.

The Crown of Aragon now committed itself firmly to a policy of
expansion in the Mediterranean. Catalan merchants embarked on the
great and hazardous venture of the spice trade with the Near East, and
in 1282 the Catalan fleet won for Aragon, after a gigantic struggle with
France and the Papacy, the kingdom of Sicily—immensely desirable
from both a strategic and trading point of view. Castile, on the other
hand, still obsessed with her mission as defender of Christian Spain,
assumed the equally expensive yet considerably less profitable role of
sentinel of the Strait of Gibraltar. It was by no means an illusory preoccupation. The end of the thirteenth century witnessed two further
Moslem invasions, albeit minor short-lived ones, and the struggle for
supremacy in the strait became almost a permanent feature of Castilian
military activities.

This Moslem pressure from Africa without and from Granada
within, inevitably led to an increase in the antagonism felt by Christians
for those Moslems who were supposedly their fellow citizens. Other,
more nebulous, pressures soon began to alienate the Christians from
the third racial group, the Jews; and in the fourteenth century the
edifice of Spain's multiracial society sadly disintegrated into hatred
and bitterness beyond repair. The history of the remainder of the Spanish Middle Ages is one in which Spain was brought rudely face to face
with the double legacy of the Reconquest—political strife due to the
sudden demobilization of a powerful nobility conditioned by and for
war, and a three-layered, unassimilated and unassimilatable, society.

CHAPTER IV

FROM RECONQUEST
TO RENAISSANCE

Following the conquest of Andalusia, Spain entered a new phase in its history, a phase characterized by the absence, for the first time in five centuries, of the "enemy" next door and Castile found herself both blessed and cursed in the accession of a new king. Blessed because culturally the reign of Alfonso X, called the Learned, was a triumph; cursed because both personally and politically it was a disaster.

The son of the great conqueror Saint Ferdinand, Alfonso (*r.* 1252–1284) was a man of enormous intellectual vision and energy; and the end, for the time being, of the crusade against the infidel allowed him the time to cultivate his scholarly passions. As his ends were too ambitious for one man to accomplish, he gathered together at Toledo a large team of scholars, translators, and scribes—Christian, Hebrew, and Arabic—to do his research and his writing for him. The enterprise, for all this, was essentially his own. He told his collaborators what he wanted, he supervised their progress, and carefully examined the results, paying special attention to language and style.

The fruit of his efforts represents a magnificent achievement that covered almost every field of human life. Instructive and imaginative

King Alfonso X, a patron of learning, dictates his Book of Chess.

works from the Near and Far East were translated and annotated. Guides to astrology, to horsemanship, and to chess were compiled. Works as disparate as a collection of songs to the Virgin Mary in Galician and a monumental history of the world were produced. But more important for Spain itself were two other works. One was the great *Estoria de Espanna* or *Primera Crónica General,* which by tracing the country's history both contributed to the development of a national consciousness and helped preserve those epic poems which were often the only source of historical information. The other was the *Siete Partidas,* a legal encyclopedia which sought to standardize the country's legislative structure and in so doing produced a fascinating digest of information of life at the time, even down to the clothes people wore. A century later the *Siete Partidas* became the law of the land.

The significance of these works lay not in what they contained alone. Alfonso's aim was to make the maximum amount of information available to the maximum number of people, and to this end the language into which his collaborators translated, and in which they wrote, was not Latin but Castilian. This meant that what was still a fairly primitive form of the vernacular, used in day-to-day living, was suddenly compelled to cope with a wide range of sophisticated subjects and abstract concepts that were entirely strange to it. In the space of this one reign, therefore, Castilian became an infinitely richer and suppler instrument of expression—a language ripe for literary development.

Alfonso's scholarly and cultural undertakings represented an enormous contribution to the intellectual foundations laid with the establishment during the previous generation of the first Spanish universities. As a result of the collaboration of Spanish, French, and Italian scholars, first Palencia in 1212, then Salamanca in about 1220, were founded in Castile. Municipal initiative and private enterprise on the part of individuals from the Church and the aristocracy ensured that these universities were subsequently supplemented by many more.

Alfonso proved himself a man of judgment, perception, and administrative ability where his learned work was concerned; however, these qualities curiously disappeared when he turned his attention to the problems of government. The sixteenth-century historian Father Juan de Mariana said of him: "He gazed so much at the sky that his crown fell off," and for centuries the traditional view of Alfonso was that of the astrologer with his head so literally in the clouds that he had no time for terrestrial matters. In fact, the opposite was true, for Alfonso's ambitions were by no means entirely academic ones. The comprehensive vision that led to such grand undertakings as a history of human civilization also led Alfonso to cast a covetous eye on the crown of the Holy Roman Empire, a claim he held through his mother. In 1256 he was nominated for the succession and the following year he was duly proclaimed emperor. The significance of the event was very great, for it indicated a new awareness in Europe of Castile as a political power. In spite of Alfonso's dream of empire, however, the time was not yet come for Castile to enter fully upon the stage of European politics. Acting in their separate interests, the pope and Alfonso's nobles compelled the king to renounce his title in 1275. In prophetic anticipation of what was to happen later on in the sixteenth and seventeenth centuries, the Castilian aristocrats feared that intervention in Europe would prove a greater drain on their country's resources than that country could bear.

Greater disappointment was on its way however, for Alfonso had to face the barons at the great turning point in their rise to political power. Hitherto the monarch had been able to employ the nobles in a cause to which they themselves were dedicated and to keep them happy with generous rewards of land. Now that Spain was to all intents and purposes Christian, this was no longer possible. The nobles were free to devote all their energies to the struggle for internal power, and with no thick layer of bourgeoisie to cushion the conflict between nobility and Crown, a confrontation was inevitable. When it came, it was all the harder for Alfonso to bear because his own son Sancho led the revolt. On the death of his eldest brother, Sancho refused to yield precedence to his brother's infant son according to the rules of strict heredity established in the *Siete Partidas*. A ferocious civil war followed which ended with the ignominious deposition of Alfonso by the Castilian Cortes (or Parliament) in 1282. The rule of might had triumphed, and the long period of sordid internal conflict that was to constitute the fourteenth and fifteenth centuries in Castile had begun. In failing to deal with his recalcitrant nobles Alfonso had set his stamp upon the remainder of the Middle Ages. Posterity alone would recognize him for the colossus he was in other, less tumultuous fields of achievement.

OVERLEAF: *In a panorama of the Inquisition, heretics are condemned in the center building, then released to secular authorities to be burned at the stake.*

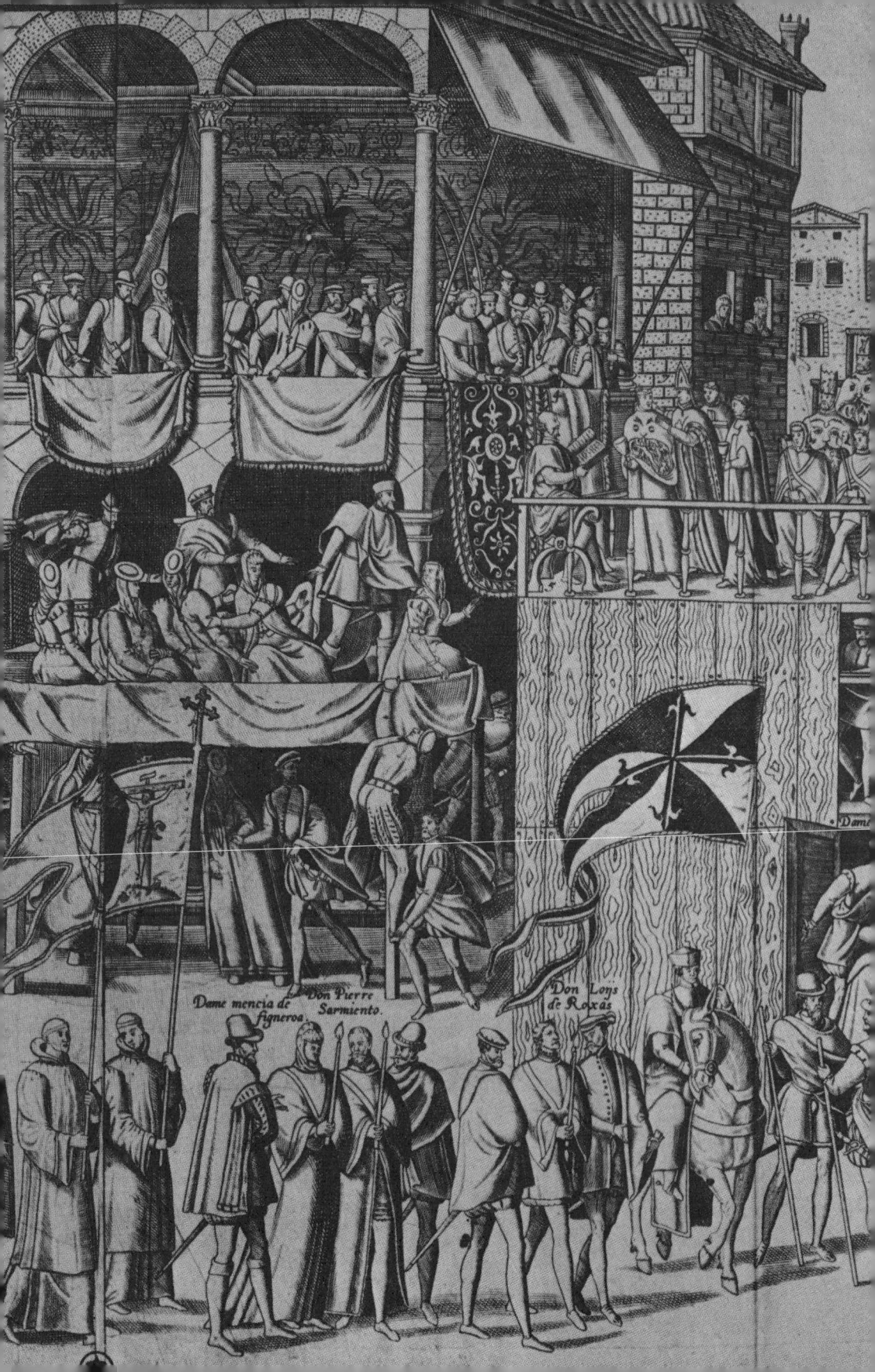

Dame mencia de
figneroa

Don Pierre
Sarmiento.

Don Loys
de Roxas

INQVISITION

Alfonso X, then, is one of the key figures of medieval Spain. But his importance is not only political and cultural. Hindsight also reveals him to have been an economic arbiter of subsequent significance. For it was Alfonso who formed "all the shepherds of Castile" into one national association called the "Honorable Assembly of the Mesta of the Shepherds," *mestas* being the name given hitherto to the groups of shepherds which met several times a year to dispose of stray sheep. In time the Mesta, which henceforth oversaw the seasonal pasturage of Spain's migratory sheep, developed into an organization of powerful vested interests controlled by the major sheep and land owners. It became the keystone of Spain's agrarian economy and an enormously effective political instrument. In the precedence it took over crop raising, it contributed, much later on, to the decline of the Spanish economy. An antagonism between the two ways of life, herding and farming, developed similar to that between the rancher and the "sodbuster" in the United States in the nineteenth century, and late in the seventeenth century the Mesta became a symbol for many of the supremacy of the rich at the cost of the poor—"What is the Mesta? It is taking money out of this purse to put into that one." So went a seventeenth-century proverb.

The decades that followed upon Alfonso's failure to control his rebellious son were troubled ones. The usurpation of the throne by Sancho IV (*r.* 1284–1295) inevitably created a legacy of conflict, of continuing opposition to himself and his heirs from those factions that held their claims to be more legitimate. The fact that Sancho's son succeeded his father when he was only nine years old served only to make matters worse, and France, Portugal, and Aragon were not slow to interfere. Fortunately the child Ferdinand grew into a fairly astute youth. As Ferdinand IV, he bought off his rivals and made alliances with his royal neighbors. Before his early death at the age of twenty-six, he found time to turn his attention to the new Moslem invaders along the south coast, and in 1312 took Gibraltar. In spite of his effectiveness, however, Castilian stability still balanced on a knife's edge. And when Ferdinand was succeeded by his year-old son, Alfonso XI, the kingdom overbalanced once more into chaos.

The outstanding figure of these years of turmoil was neither a king nor a troublesome noble, but a woman. If Sancho IV left behind him a

legacy of political woe, he also left a consort who was to prove the
kingdom's lifeline through the minorities of her son and grandson.
Queen María de Molina alone held her country together when King
Sancho died and his nobles turned like a pack of ravening wolves upon
his young heir. Even the towns seized this opportunity to oppose a
succession they regarded as illegitimate. That María was able to hold
her son's enemies at bay until he had come of age was a remarkable
achievement indeed in that rough and warlike age of men, and is an
eloquent testimony both to her authority and her guile. On the death of
her son seventeen years later she again stepped in to save the throne
for her infant grandson. When he too came of age she retired once
more into the decent obscurity of conventional widowhood. The very
stuff of which legend is made, this great woman soon entered the
annals of Spain's history as one of its most popular heroines. Whatever
the origin of the royal line for which she fought, she stood for social
and political stability. But it was as the epitome of female perfection
that she captured the imagination of the Spaniards in centuries to come.
Later on, voicing qualms and fears inspired in his generation by the
accession of the young Philip IV in 1621, the dramatist Tirso de Molina
immortalized her in *La prudencia en la mujer,* a splendid play that
depicts María de Molina in her three-fold glory as perfect wife, mother,
and sovereign. There could be no worthier tribute than this drama to
a great queen and a remarkable woman.

Her grandson's reign is memorable for the renewed struggle with
Islam. The continuing chaos within Castile was an open invitation for
Granada to step in, bringing its allies, the Marinids, who had risen to
power in Morocco in the thirteenth century. And once again the Moslems crossed the strait. But eventually Alfonso XI won a conclusive
victory over the invaders with the help of Aragon and Portugal. It was
at this Battle of Río Salado in 1340 that artillery was used perhaps
for the first time in Europe. Four years later Alfonso, with the help of
Chaucer's knight and many more foreign crusaders, besieged and
captured Algeciras. Spain would not be invaded again until Napoleon's
armies marched into the Peninsula.

The continuing conflict between the Castilian Crown and nobility
came to a dramatic head at the end of the next reign. According to
legend, and in this case legend may well be right, the struggle was

theatrically symbolized—and the climax actually realized—with a terrible hand-to-hand fight to the death between King Peter and his bastard half brother, Henry of Trastamara. Peter the Cruel—or the Dispenser of Justice as he was alternatively known depending on the interests involved—was an able and determined king whose reign was dogged by misfortune. Under him, Castile, seriously debilitated by constant civil strife, began to make an impressive economic recovery only to be devastated by famine and the Black Death, which hit Spain in waves from the middle of the fourteenth century on. More to the point, he possessed no fewer than five jealous illegitimate brothers. And when Peter attempted to secure his own position and cure the ills of his kingdom by curbing the political and economic power of the landed aristocracy, these rival siblings, of whom the eldest was Henry of Trastamara, led the revolt against him.

The situation became high drama as Peter earned his less flattering title by ruthlessly disposing of all those who intrigued to separate him from his crown—brothers, cousins, an archbishop, even, perhaps, his own queen. The conflict, moreover, became an international one. France and Aragon sided with Henry. England and Navarre sided with Peter. Both sides sent their champions to the fight. From France came Bertrand du Guesclin, head of the mercenary adventurers called White Companies, and cast by Spanish legend as the villain of the piece. From England came Edward, the Black Prince, mainly attracted by the idea of measuring himself against the famous Du Guesclin. Edward eventually became disenamored with Peter and his cause, and returned to England, bearing the spinel that became known as the Black Prince's ruby when it took pride of place in the English crown. The jewel, after the manner of so many great gems, has a history of evil. For in order to get it Peter the Cruel is said to have brutally and treacherously murdered his ally, the king of Granada. Certainly it brought the Castilian king no luck. On a dark night in 1369, in a tent pitched outside the castle of Montiel in Extremadura, Peter was surprised by an intruder and murdered. Whether the intruder was Henry, as legend assures us, or a hired assassin, has never been finally ascertained, but there seems little doubt that morally the crime was Henry's. He had clearly decided to resolve the conflict by striking at its very source.

Nothing was solved by Henry's triumph. Brute force had again won the day and a pair of bloodstained hands had seized the crown. The new house of Trastamara had come into being with the help of the nobles and was therefore indebted to them. They were rewarded with new grants of land, and with further financial privileges. These concessions stimulated rather than satisfied the power-lust of the nobility, and the seemingly endless and meaningless civil wars continued.

These years from the death of Saint Ferdinand in the middle of the thirteenth century to the succession of Isabella in the second half of the fifteenth century were dark days for Castile. Like the Wars of the Roses in England they were a long and painful prelude to the emergence of a firmly established, autocratic, monarchy. The Crown of Aragon in the meantime was coping rather better with the aftermath of the Reconquest. A healthier economy, based, unlike Castile's, on commerce and industry, enabled it to withstand more easily the upheavals created by its nobles. Sardinia was pacified, Catalan maritime trade for a while enjoyed a success rivaled only by that of Venice or Genoa, and the resulting prosperity encouraged the growth of a rich urban patriciate. The economic power wielded by this dense bourgeoisie enabled the Crown to challenge successfully the growing demands of the Aragonese aristocracy and contain its power and privileges within the formal limits established in the past.

The major source of social unrest in Aragon, in fact, was not the nobility. On the contrary, when real trouble came it emanated from the other end of the social scale, from the peasants who formed the base of Catalan's feudal system. When famine and the Black Death exacerbated the depression caused by a decline in Catalan prosperity after the fourteenth century, there sprang up a widespread agrarian conflict between the laborers, who suddenly found themselves in a strong bargaining position, and their landlords, who continued to insist nevertheless on their ancient privileges—the "evil customs," as they became known. The great surge toward the shining goal of emancipation that was the outcome of this conflict was to culminate in the seventeenth century in the "Revolt of the Catalans."

For centuries the Christian kingdoms had found their identity and their directing purpose in war against an ever-present and easily distinguishable enemy. Now they were wrestling with the thornier problems —political, social, and economic—of a period of nominal peace in

Spanish shepherds, as depicted in a religion-inspired miniature of 1468

which the enemies were to be found within their own gates. But in
spite of the teething troubles that beset the slow progress toward some
sort of maturity, the complex patterns of everyday life lent an increasingly richer texture to society at all levels. Released from their crusading duties the peasant tilled in peace, the craftsman joined his guild,
and the nobleman became a courtier. Not least, the foundations of
Spain's splendid national literature were laid.

Although lyric poetry is now known to have been the first vehicle for
literature written in the vernacular instead of in Latin, it was the Castilian epic, written by anonymous *jongleurs* for recitation in the market
place and before the fireside, that embodied the rude, warlike spirit of
emergent Christianity in the Peninsula. The *Cantar de mío Cid* is the
one surviving epic of any size. As time went on the epic would seem to
have been transformed into the shorter, snappier ballad, likewise tied
in its earlier days to the contemporary struggles of Spain. Some of the
most vivid of these *romances*—as ballads are called in Spanish—deal
with the border disputes with Granada and with the dark, titanic
struggle between Peter the Cruel and his half brother Henry. It is
interesting, however, that formal literature in Spain only came into
existence once the Reconquest was virtually accomplished, that is, from
the thirteenth century on. And Alfonso the Learned's example gave
these formal beginnings an enormous boost. His 417 *Songs of the
Virgin Mary* constitute Spain's first body of lyric verse. The ballads
aside, literature now became largely the pastime of scholars and cour-
tiers instead of the daily living of professional versemakers, and it was
now that writers began to think seriously enough of their work to leave
their names attached to their compositions. The greatest of these names
belongs to the century after Alfonso—the fourteenth. Juan Ruiz' *Book
of Good Love* is the outstanding work of the Spanish Middle Ages, a
work comparable in breadth, humor, naughtiness, and indeed in stature, to the *Canterbury Tales*. A glorious mix of songs, prayers, fables,
allegories, parodies, and tales of seduction in a variety of verse forms,
it appears to exalt carnal love while claiming to recommend only love
of God. The real purpose of the author—often called the "archpriest
of Hita"—if he had one, still remains a mystery.

It was in the fifteenth century, however, that medieval Spanish literature reached its full flowering as new influences from abroad began

to be felt. The sordid civil wars of the fourteenth century continued unabated as an infant, John II (1405–1454), succeeded to the throne of Castile. John grew up into a weak monarch, ruled by a favorite who in his turn became a focus for aristocratic jealousy and discontent as he fought for the supremacy of the Crown. But the king also grew up to become a patron of the arts and was himself a cultured man, prepared to hand over his sovereign duties in favor of his lute. John's court became the center of scholarly and creative activity. His favorite, Alvaro de Luna, and one of his noblest opponents, the Marquis of Santillana, were amongst those who cultivated the literary exercise of courtly love and tried their hand at the new forms, themes, and meters that came from Italy with the works of Dante, Petrarch, and Boccaccio.

This flourishing cultural life, unfortunately, was the sugar coating on an increasingly bitter pill. For now the turmoil of the preceding centuries came to an explosive head as Spain shared in that crisis that gripped a Europe beset by economic depression and torn between the deocentric values of the Middle Ages and the humanist values of the Renaissance. An interrupted line of succession had put Castile and Aragon in the hands of a common dynasty at the beginning of the century, and this inevitably led to endless interference of each kingdom in the affairs of the other. As luck would have it, the kings dealt to Aragon were able and strong, while those dealt to Castile were the most disastrous in a disastrous line of sovereigns. John II, who died regretting that he "had not been born the son of a mechanic instead of king of Castile," was followed by his son Henry IV (r. 1454–1474) who was both incompetent and impotent, a combination unforgivable in a monarch. It says much for the inner strength and vitality of Castile that it was to emerge from this unfavorable contest as the dominant partner of the two. John's Aragonese counterpart, Alfonso V (r. 1416–1458), for his part, became so enamored of the spirit of Renaissance Italy that after he became king of Naples in 1443 he transferred his court there and made of it one of the most scintillating centers of cultural activity in Europe. This close connection with Naples was to prove of consummate importance in Spain's cultural evolution.

The Reconquest's twofold legacy of aristocratic unrest and religious intolerance reached fruition in these years. The power-hungry barons made last, desperate attempts to consolidate their position; attempts

which led to the execution in 1453 of Alvaro de Luna and later on in
1465 to the dethronement in effigy of Henry IV and the proclamation
of his young half brother, Alfonso, as king. Yet more sinister, however,
was the growing climate of religious and racial disharmony. The considerable degree of coexistence achieved in the past began to yield
before new pressures, and in the fourteenth century the pogroms began
in earnest. As far as the Jews were concerned, the end came much later
in Spain than elsewhere, for they had already been expelled from most
countries in Europe and their influence eliminated from the major
money marts outside of Spain. In Castile the Crown was for a long
time reluctant to put any stamp of official approval on popular anti-
Semitism because in the absence of a developed capitalistic economy
centered on banking, the monarchs relied on Jewish money to finance
their enterprises. And not only monarchs, but towns, nobles, military
orders, even the Church, had to submit to Jewish financial control. This
inevitably increased the envy and embitterment of the indebted Christian community a thousandfold, and only a financial crisis was
needed to fan the smoldering embers into a raging fire.

The crisis came with the economic depression at the end of the
fourteenth century. In 1391 the growing religious fanaticism exploded
into a terrible chain of massacres, though other ugly motives were also
involved—"all this was more out of thirst for robbery than out of
devotion," as a chronicler of the day remarked. In June of that year
four thousand Jews were slaughtered in Seville alone. The alternative
to persecution was forced conversion and this was a way out that many
Jews took. But the outcome was only increased hostility, increased
suspicion. Jews had been vulnerable and easily recognizable; *conversos*
wore the protective coloring of an apparent Christianity and took their
wealth and influence with them into the new religion. It was now in
the fifteenth century that the obsession with *limpieza de sangre,* purity
of blood, first put its noxious grip on Spanish society. The fact that the
Christianization of rich and influential Jewish families had made them
eligible for marriage with established and high-ranking Christian families complicated a situation already fraught with suspicion, and by the
end of the century made a nonsense of the very concept of "purity of
blood" in the higher levels of society. Greed and ambition overcame
scruples to produce an ethnically mixed community. Four of Queen

Isabella's bishops, two of her secretaries, her confessor, and the grand masters of the military orders of Santiago and Calatrava, were of *converso* descent, while in Aragon few noble families were without some Jewish blood, and Ferdinand himself was thought to have Jewish ancestors. Nevertheless, the fiction of purity was cultivated with unholy zeal. After centuries of fighting the infidel, nobility had become identified in the Peninsula with Christianity—many aristocrats owed their titles, their lands, their wealth, to the fervor with which they had forwarded the cause of the "true faith." Here our two strands of conflict—a mixed society and an unruly aristocracy—merge. The old Christian aristocracy feared and resented the challenge to their political power represented by Jewish financiers and by the increasing band of influential *converso* intellectuals and administrators. They fanned religious intolerance amongst the populace and pressured the Crown to introduce racist legislation. Animosity toward Jews induced a frame of mind which despised all religious and racial aliens, Moors included, and since the Moors were the industrious members of society, that scorn for work which was to gnaw at the vitals of Spain's well-being like some monstrous worm in succeeding centuries, was born.

From 1412 on, official discrimination of a serious social nature was introduced. Practicing Jews and Moors were forbidden to hold office or titles, to bear arms, to hire Christians, to follow certain trades. They might not even talk to Christians and were compelled to identify themselves clearly with rough clothing and long hair and beards. In 1473 all *conversos* were forcibly expelled from Córdoba, and in the outbreak of murders that followed, the constable of Castile, a *converso* of the highest eminence, was killed in front of a church altar at Jaén.

The double legacy of the Reconquest had come home to roost in a social and political crisis of gigantic proportions. The monarchy was debased and beleaguered by a seemingly uncontrollable aristocracy, and the fabric of society was falling apart at the seams. Only the imposition of authority and unity could save Castile from utter chaos, and such a cure must at times have appeared inconceivable. Yet cure there was. The physicians were Isabella, queen of Castile, and Ferdinand, king of Aragon, who as husband and wife created modern Spain and, with their hands firmly on the wheel of state, steered the course that was to lead their country to world supremacy.

On October 19, 1469, before the altar of a private house in Valladolid, Princess Isabella, eighteen-year-old half sister of Henry IV of
Castile, was joined in matrimony by the archbishop of Toledo to the
seventeen-year-old heir to the Crown of Aragon, Ferdinand. They were
an impressive pair. Ferdinand was comely, athletic, and tough, a youth
molded by war and physical exercise, whose shrewd, native intelligence
amply compensated for a limited education. His plump, sweet-faced
bride was dignified, well-educated for her day, and extremely devout.
From her blue-green Trastamara eyes there shone already an authority
and resolution that had led her, against the wishes of her brother, the
king, to the considered choice of Ferdinand from among her many
suitors. For Spain the choice was a momentous one in that it determined
once and for all the future pattern of the Peninsula. For centuries the

*The kingdoms and provinces of the Iberian Peninsula during the reign of
Ferdinand and Isabella*

Peninsula had been divided into three kingdoms—Castile, Aragon, and Portugal. When the grandson of Ferdinand and Isabella eventually inherited both their crowns, that number would be reduced to two—Portugal and Castile-Aragon, or Spain, as the latter became known to the world. The possibility of a different division, with a Castile-Portugal complex and an independent Aragon, had been at the time a very real one. Not only because Isabella might have chosen as her husband the king of Portugal, a man twice her age, but because the royal succession in Castile itself was in dispute. Henry IV had brought the reputation of the monarchy to its lowest ebb. Not only had his apathy and mismanagement encouraged the spread of corruption and crime and created a financial crisis which ground the poor into the dust, but he was apparently incapable even of producing an heir. When his second wife, Joanna of Portugal, eventually did give birth, Henry was dismissed as a cuckold as well, for the child was thought by all to be the daughter not of Henry but of Henry's favorite, Beltrán de la Cueva. She was accordingly known all her life as Joanna la Beltraneja.

The doubts about the younger Joanna's paternity—now thought by many to have been unfounded—gave rise to full-scale civil war. The Castilian nobles, always eager for a pretext to challenge the authority of the Crown, refused to accept Joanna as Henry's heir and proclaimed his half brother Alfonso heir instead. When in 1468 Alfonso, a healthy fourteen-year-old, was found dead in his bed, Joanna la Beltraneja and Alfonso's sister Isabella found themselves rivals to the throne. Isabella's marriage to Ferdinand antagonized many of her supporters and sent them over to Joanna's side. On the death of Henry in 1474 they offered Joanna and the Castilian throne to the Portuguese king whom Isabella had refused. The Portuguese armies immediately entered Castile and the Peninsula went to war to decide its future.

Meanwhile, Isabella proclaimed herself Queen of Castile, and two days later the twenty-three-year-old queen received the homage of her people at Segovia. Five years later, after a long struggle during which Isabella often personally supervised her campaigns and gradually won the vast majority of Castilians to her flag, Portugal renounced all rights to the throne of Castile and Joanna entered the convent of Santa Clara at Coimbra. At twenty-eight Isabella was undisputed queen. In that same year, John II of Aragon died and his son succeeded him as Ferdinand II. The joint sovereignty of the Catholic monarchs had begun.

It was a reign which future Spaniards were to look back at with the same sort of fond nostalgia that the reign of Elizabeth I inspires in Englishmen, with a similar feeling that it was their country's moment of greatest vitality. And a remarkable reign it was in every way. Spain was united and pacified, the authority of the Crown became absolute, the country assumed its full role in the arena of European politics and diplomacy, Granada was finally conquered, religious orthodoxy was imposed, and a whole New World was discovered. Furthermore, Isabella's enthusiasm for the new learning of the Renaissance infused the kingdom with renewed cultural activity. The period was at once a culmination and a beginning.

The royal partnership was a complex and successful one. Each kingdom retained its sovereignty under its own monarch, and each monarch perpetuated the traditions, interests, and attitudes of his own kingdom, Isabella's policy being a centralist one concerned with home affairs, Ferdinand's a federal one interested in the Mediterranean and the wider European scene. Nonetheless, Castile gradually and inexorably emerged as the dominant partner. This was perhaps in part due to the very fact that it was Isabella who took charge of internal affairs, but there were more tangible reasons. Castile was larger and more densely populated, while the Crown of Aragon had been seriously affected by the decline of Catalonia. More directly significant, the power of the monarchy was not constitutionally limited in Castile as it was in Aragon and Navarre—Aragonese subjects agreed to accept the rule of their king according to the following conditions: "We who are as good as you swear to you who are no better than we, to accept you as our king and sovereign lord, provided you accept all our liberties and laws; but if not, not." That the royal will could be put into effect with comparative impunity in Castile led the Catholic Monarchs to center their activities there. And the fact that Ferdinand was Castilian bred and Isabella a stranger to Aragon made the choice doubly natural.

The first task that confronted Isabella on her succession was that of subduing the nobles. Isabella's procedure was one of compromise. Monarchic authoritarianism was imposed, the nobility were prevented from meddling arbitrarily in high affairs of State, and control of the military orders was systematically acquired by the Crown. On the other

hand, the nobles' wealth, territorial possessions, and privileges were confirmed. In other words, their power was consolidated but kept under control. Inevitably the consolidation of their privileges involved the consolidation of those of the Mesta, with which the nobles were by now so closely involved economically. The result was that grain production eventually failed to meet the needs of the population, with all that this meant in terms of a threat, from then on, of famine.

The stabilization and pacification of society produced by the quelling of the nobles and by the ruthless burning to the ground of all fortresses and castles deemed unnecessary for the nation's defense—fifty were razed in Galicia alone—was completed with the reintroduction of an institution that had fallen into disuse: the *Santa Hermandad,* or Holy Brotherhood. This became a primitive rural police force with powers of summary justice throughout the open countryside. The appalling crime level of the previous reign rapidly fell as offenders were hunted down and harshly punished. The ordering of society thus achieved was accomplished by changes which almost at a stroke transformed Castile from a medieval into a recognizably modern state. Administration was centralized and a civil service created for the purpose of running it. Official posts were distributed on merit and qualifications instead of wealth and influence. The advent of professional, university-educated, middle-class administrators helped prize the great nobles from their position of capricious control in state affairs. From 1480 the Royal Council was composed, very largely, of these "new men"—and they even began to challenge the lords in other capacities, such as the practice of literature. The fact that many of these counselors, secretaries, and lawyers were *conversos* did nothing to help the by now red-hot atmosphere of religious hatred.

Isabella was as intent on uniting her people as she was on pacifying them. The situation she had inherited was one of suspicion and extreme animosity with an obvious cause—religion. Heterodoxy seemed to be polluting the very air of Castile. The populace hated the unbelievers, the bishops and nobles resented and feared their influence. While they continued to exist on Spanish soil, conversion itself would remain doubly suspect. The Church ranted, the aristocracy pressured, and Isabella, pious and with the welfare of her kingdom at heart, saw no alternative, certainly no worthier alternative, to the seething unrest,

Opposite: above, coat of arms of Castile and Aragon, joined through marriage in 1469; below, polychrome wooden statues of Ferdinand and Isabella

than the imposition of religious orthodoxy. Upon it depended political unity and social stability, and what better aim anyway for a devout daughter of God?

Not all Spanish Christians were intent on persecution; Alonso Carrillo, the archbishop of Toledo who had officiated at the royal wedding, remarked, "Divisions bring great scandals and schism and divide the seamless garment of Christ, who, as the Good Shepherd, commanded us to love one another in unity and obedience to Holy Mother Church. . . . From which it is obvious how culpable are those who . . . create different lineages, some calling themselves Old Christians and others calling themselves New Christians or Conversos." But the enlightened few were powerless in the face of the prejudice and self-interest of the major part of Castilian society. The *conversos* were the first to be dealt with. Isabella with some reluctance gave way before the exhortations of Church fathers such as her early confessor, the fanatical Tomás de Torquemada, and in 1478 asked permission of the pope to introduce into Castile an inquisition that would persecute heresy and enforce religious orthodoxy. She intended it to be a means of guiding back into the Church through penance those *conversos* who had relapsed into their former religious practices. In reality, it was in the early years an instrument of racial persecution. In time, the Inquisition was to develop into an arm of the Spanish government, controlled and answerable to the Crown, and organized on a procedure of anonymous accusation, which created round the Inquisition an aura of horror, cruelty, and refinements of torture that the rather less lurid facts uncovered by recent investigations will never be able to dispel. On February 6, 1481, the first auto-da-fé in the history of the Spanish Inquisition took place in Seville. After a solemn procession and sermon, six prisoners found guilty of heresy and unwilling to repent were turned over to the secular authorities and burned at the stake. The foundation stone for the "black legend" of repression, cruelty, and fear that was to damn Spain in the eyes of Europe in centuries to come had been laid.

With the religiously insincere thus attended to, the Catholic Monarchs turned their eyes to that surviving insult to Christianity on Spanish soil, the Moorish kingdom of Granada. From the Christian point of view, Granada was dangerous: it was a focus for the hopes of persecuted *Moriscos*—Christianized Moors—and for the ambitions of the

Moslem Turks who were fast overrunning the Mediterranean. Indeed,
it was Granada that first broke the truce. In 1476 King Mulay Hassan replied to Ferdinand and Isabella's demand for payment of the annual tribute that "the mints of Granada coined no longer gold, but steel." Five years later the Moorish armies attacked the Christian fortress of Zahara on the Andalusian frontier and carried off every surviving man, woman, and child into slavery in Granada. By this time Ferdinand and Isabella had put in order the affairs of their own kingdom, and they seized the opportunity offered them by the broken truce to undertake a campaign to drive the Moors from their land forever, and finally exact revenge for the great invasion seven and a half centuries before.

Their attack began in 1482. The Christians waged an arduous campaign during which Ferdinand rode at the head of his armies while Isabella acted as financier and quartermaster, on one occasion marching south to join her troops though heavily pregnant with her fourth child. In 1491 the Christian forces, fifty thousand strong, camped on the *vega* below the capital city, Granada itself. In October of that year, terms began to be discussed, Ferdinand promising religious freedom in return for the surrender of the new Moorish king, Mohammed XI. And on the morning of January 2, 1492, Mohammed (called Boabdil by the Spaniards) and fifty of his cavaliers rode through the gates of the Alhambra and down through its gardens to the banks of the river Genil where Ferdinand and Isabella waited. There he handed over the keys of his citadel. Shortly afterward a great silver cross appeared on the battlements and four days later the Catholic Monarchs received the homage of their new subjects in the Alhambra's splendid throne room. Later that month church bells all over rang out in joyous celebration of the news that Spain was, officially, once again a wholly Christian country. That same year saw the expulsion from Spain of all Jews not prepared to abjure their faith. And in the following year the pope rewarded the royal pair's service to the faith by bestowing upon them the title *Los reyes católicos*—the Catholic Monarchs.

The Inquisition, the conquest of Granada, the expulsion of the Jews, spelled out their policy and their determination—unity and conformity would be imposed whatever the effort, whatever the cost. That the immediate goal was social stability rather than religious orthodoxy is illustrated by the fact that ten years were to pass before Spain's other

religious minority—the Moriscos—was subjected to the same treatment. But the religious temperature inevitably mounted and the fact that the choice of expulsion or conversion imposed upon the Jews had made a potential fifth column of the whole of remaining Spanish Jewry did not help matters. In Granada the promise of religious freedom was not honored for long. In 1499 the zealous Cardinal Francisco Jiménez de Cisneros went to Granada and inaugurated a program of ferocious proselytization. In one day he baptized three thousand Moors in a mass ceremony; on another he ceremoniously committed to a public bonfire all the Arabic books and manuscripts he could lay his hands on, virtually destroying Arabic scholarship in Spain. The result was a short-lived Moorish revolt which led Ferdinand to remark scathingly to the queen, "So we are like to pay dear for your Archbishop, whose rashness has lost us in a few hours what we have been years in acquiring." But Cisneros prevailed, and the people of Granada were given the alternatives of baptism or exile. In 1502 Isabella completed her services to God with the expulsion of the Moors from all Castile. In Aragon, on the other hand, an awareness of the Moslems' usefulness as a source of cheap labor prevailed—*"mientras más moros, más ganancia,"* "the more Moors, the more profit"—and Ferdinand warned the Aragonese inquisitors to leave them in peace. They survived there until 1525.

The year 1492 was a landmark in Spain's history. For the first time men from every region had fought as a united country under a single leader. The Spanish armies had learned military tactics and discipline, laying the foundation for an infantry which was in the next century to become famous all over Europe. Now that Moslem Spain had been conquered, the Spaniards would carry the crusading ideal which had become for them a national mission into North Africa itself. More important for the world, among the crowds that cheered the sovereigns' triumphant entry into Granada on January 6 of that memorable year, stood the son of a Genoese wool weaver, called Christopher Columbus.

Columbus had already pleaded his cause before the Portuguese, who, since the time of their brilliant young prince, Henry the Navigator, had been engaged in a program of exploration and discovery. But they were not convinced by the red-haired, blue-eyed visionary who claimed that given financial support he could sail to the Orient, heartland of the spice trade, by sailing west. He had first sought Spanish help in

King James I presiding over the Cortes in the town of Lérida

1486, but not until three months after the fall of Granada did Isabella, riding high on Spain's newest triumph and obsessed with the vision of an expanding, crusading nation, reach a decision. To her everlasting credit, she claimed the enterprise of the Indies for Castile.

On August 3 of that momentous year the *Niña,* the *Pinta,* and the *Santa María* put out to sea from Palos on the Atlantic coast. Eight months later, Columbus walked into the royal court in Barcelona accompanied by six Indian natives and laden with pearls, gold masks, strange fruits, and exotic parrots, and at the feet of Ferdinand and Isabella laid, without realizing it, not the Orient but a new world, a vast empire in the Western Hemisphere which would for a time make Spain master of Europe. The most splendid chapter in Spain's history had opened. And thanks to the leadership of Ferdinand and Isabella, Spain was ready for it.

The reign of Ferdinand and Isabella witnessed a spectacular widening of Spain's horizons in every direction. A united nation in the eyes of the world if not yet entirely in her own, she now fixed her gaze on the world about her, not only south to Africa and west to the Indies but east and north as well. Castile took Spain across the ocean, and Aragon involved her in Europe and the Mediterranean. The struggle over Sicily and Naples had already made enemies of Aragon and France, and the continuation of this struggle under Ferdinand—whose true interests lay in European politics—initiated two centuries of hostilities between Spain and her great northern neighbor. Ferdinand's mastery of diplomacy—that led many to think him the source of Machiavelli's Prince—won him Cerdagne and Roussillon within the Peninsula, then Naples and the whole of southern Italy that went with it. When diplomacy failed, he fell back on an army with a growing reputation, acquired during the Italian wars under the command of the Great Captain, Gonzalo Fernández de Córdoba. This army wrested Navarre from the grip of France in 1512 and incorporated it permanently into Castile. And of course, as well as a gift for diplomacy and a powerful army, Ferdinand had a third card up his sleeve—four daughters and a son. These he used to cement alliances to encircle France and provide for a variety of contingencies. In an attempt to secure Portugal, Isabella the eldest daughter was married twice over into that country, first to the heir to the throne, and then two years after,

Boabdil, El Chico (the Little), who surrendered Granada to the Catholic Monarchs in 1492, thus ending the era of Moslem domination in Spain

EL REY, CHYCO, D GRANAD

when she was widowed, to her late husband's uncle, now king. The Burgundy-Austria front was doubly secured by the marriage of the Catholic Monarchs' heir, Prince John, to the Hapsburg Princess Margaret of Austria, and by that of his sister, Princess Joanna, to Philip the Fair of Burgundy. Catherine of Aragon was dispatched to England where she became the unfortunate first wife of Henry VIII. But even Ferdinand could not command the unruly forces of life and death, and these ambitious plans for his family were brought to nought by a series of tragedies which drove Queen Isabella to her grave. Prince John died at seventeen and his wife gave birth a few months later to a stillborn child. The following year, Isabella of Portugal died in childbirth and was survived not two years by her baby son. Joanna, now heiress, lost her reason, and Catherine of Aragon was divorced by Henry Tudor. The creators of modern Spain would not be followed by a Spaniard to the throne.

With the Catholic Monarchs Spain was at once born and come of age, entering fully into its new role as a world power. It is almost impossible to exaggerate their importance to Spanish history in all areas of activity, internal and external, political and military, social and religious. The Spain of the sixteenth century was a nation in whose shaping they had played a major part, both for good and for evil. The success of Ferdinand and Isabella lay largely in the fact that between them both, their interest in Spain was a totally comprehensive one. They wanted their country to be great and they realized that true greatness lay in no one direction alone. They were eager at once to preserve and defend the best values of Christian Spain's past and to put their nation in the forefront of modern Europe. And these attitudes were summed up in Isabella's reaction to the Renaissance.

Her son was given the best education money could buy, and her daughters were taught by two leading humanists—Antonio and Alessandro Geraldini—brought from Italy for the purpose. Early in her reign Isabella gave Spanish printers special tax exemptions as encouragement, and all duties were removed from books entering the country from abroad. Scholars flowed into Spain, chairs of Hebrew and Greek were established at Salamanca, which rapidly became one of the chief centers of European learning, and a new university was planned for Alcalá de Henares. Classical and Italian works were translated into

Spanish. Eager to keep abreast of developments, Isabella in middle age
even set to learning Latin.

Spanish literature itself received an enormous boost from this atmosphere of renewed vitality as well as from the advent of printing. The vogue for courtly love reached its climax in the sentimental romances and songbooks of the age—much of the poetry being directed at Isabella herself; that for the chivalresque romance took on a new lease of life in Spain with the publication in 1508 of *Amadís de Gaula.* And in 1499 there appeared Fernando de Rojas' *La Celestina,* a novel in dialogue form, which, with its realism and its tremendous pace, is often hailed as the mother of the modern European novel. Telling of a pair of ill-fated lovers and the bawd that brought them together, the author, in the name of human dignity and reason, rejected that concept of idealized love between man and woman that had dictated the sentimental attitudes of noble minds of Europe since the twelfth century, and thereby closed a door on the past.

What distinguished Isabella's enthusiasm for the new learning was that in her eyes educational and cultural innovation was inseparably linked with religious reform. And her invaluable supporter in the task of fostering culture and learning in Spain, Cardinal Cisneros, agreed with her. A program of disciplinary reform was undertaken which anticipated the Reformation, and while the Italian Renaissance was characterized by nonreligious, even pagan, tendencies, in Spain there was an increase in religious poetry and a revival of religious scholarship. Isabella died in 1504. Ferdinand was to live twelve more years. According to the court observer Peter Martyr, the world had lost in Isabella "its noblest ornament"; Cisneros carried on their work alone. Together they ensured that Spain took from the Renaissance only what it needed, what was appropriate to her history and to her destiny as they saw them. Between them they ensured that the Spanish Renaissance took a course that would make a Spanish Reformation almost impossible.

CHAPTER V

IMPERIAL SPAIN

September 17, 1517, a Flemish youth of sixteen set foot for the first time on Spanish soil. On November 1 of that same year, a middle-aged German theologian nailed his ninety-five theses to the door of Wittenberg Cathedral. The boy was Spain's new king, Charles I, soon to become Charles V of the Holy Roman Empire—the title by which he is known to posterity. The theologian was Martin Luther, reformer of the Christian Church. In April, 1521, they confronted each other at the Diet of Worms in Germany. Charles pledged his dominions, his life, his soul, to the defense of Christendom. Luther presented a defense of his doctrines which resulted in his being outlawed from the empire. Between them these men were to affect profoundly the path of European history, for they were the major contenders in that mammoth struggle for the soul of Europe which was to rend Christendom forever in two.

Thanks to the timely reforms of Isabella and Cisneros, Spain internally was to remain comparatively unaffected by the spiritual conflict as such; what leanings there were toward unorthodoxy were countered with swift and repressive measures. But the imperial ambitions and

The Holy Roman Emperor Charles V is shown here in a 1548 portrait by Titian.

obligations it took on when it acquired Charles as king, sucked the nation inevitably and remorselessly into the political and military maelstrom that the Reformation resolved itself into in Germany and the Netherlands.

Charles, grandson of Ferdinand and Isabella, succeeded to the thrones of Castile and Aragon on the death of Ferdinand in 1516. His mother, poor Joanna the Mad, was deemed unfit to rule. When he arrived in Spain, Charles spoke not a word of Spanish, and the antagonism this naturally inspired in his subjects was made far worse by his initial highhandedness in sharing out the choice positions in the land among his Flemish favorites. The enormously rich archbishopric of Toledo, the Spanish primate's see, was given to a boy who had not even left his native Flanders. But worse was to come. In 1519 Charles' paternal grandfather, the Hapsburg Emperor Maximilian I, died. To the dismay of a Spain which saw itself being relegated to second place in its sovereign's priorities, Charles managed to bribe his way to the Hapsburg imperial throne, adding Austria, Tyrol, and parts of southern Germany to his dominions. He left immediately for Germany, already in debt after the expensive election and in possession of loans he had succeeded in squeezing out of the Spanish Mesta and a reluctant Cortes. The pattern for the coming years had already been set—an absentee king draining Spanish resources in pursuit of enterprises that were not properly Spain's own. This financial, human, and emotional investment in Europe was to continue for almost two hundred years, and become the major reason for Spain's eventual decline.

But this is the blacker side of the picture of Charles' relationship with Spain, and there is a golden one. Indeed Charles' reign initiates that period in Spanish history and culture known as the Golden Age. And if politically the term can hardly be regarded as appropriate of the seventeenth century as well as the sixteenth, so far as literature and the arts are concerned the word "golden" can never have been more aptly applied than to the century and a half that followed upon Charles' involvement with the empire and Europe. In painting, this period gave the world Murillo, El Greco, and Velázquez; in sculpture Berruguete, and in architecture the New Cathedral at Salamanca, the Renaissance palace in the Alhambra, the University of Alcalá de Henares near Madrid, the cathedral erected plumb in the middle of the Great Mosque at Córdoba, the Escorial, the sacristy of the Charterhouse of Granada, and other splendid churches and palaces too numerous to mention.

In literature it produced works of a quality and quantity which have never been surpassed. The poets, prose writers, and dramatists form a glittering constellation of genius which triumphed later even over the hermetically sealed atmosphere of Counter-Reformation and post-Counter-Reformation Spain: Garcilaso de la Vega, Saint John of the Cross, Saint Teresa de Ávila, Fray Luis de León, Cervantes, Lope de Vega, Tirso de Molina, Góngora, Quevedo, Calderón de la Barca, and Gracián—all are figures of world stature. Spain at this time gave the world the picaresque novel *Don Quijote* and, in the greatest out-pouring of dramatic writing the world has ever known, an endless source for theatrical imitation inside and outside of Spain.

Culturally, involvement in Europe proved beneficial to Spain. Riding high on the glorious legacies of the previous reign, the country gradu-ally yielded to the lure of imperial power and learned to espouse the causes of her king. Charles in his turn underwent an insidious meta-morphosis that instilled in him a strong sense of Spain's religious mission as well as a propensity to regard Spanish as his first language. The country's new sense of imperial destiny encouraged cultural ex-change and an awareness of the outside world, while Charles' gradual acclimatization to Spanish attitudes did not prevent his being for many years a keen supporter of reform and an advocate of a "European" Spain. After the death of Cisneros in 1517, the Dutch theologian Eras-mus became the main influence behind Charles' religious policy. The king's secretary of state was Alfonso de Valdés who, with his brother Juan, was one of the leading Erasmian humanists. And when in 1527 Charles' German army sacked Rome without his permission and made the pope a prisoner, Alfonso de Valdés was only one of many who re-garded the event as a providential opportunity to abolish the temporal power of the papacy and establish a purer, truly spiritual Christianity. Valdés' *Dialogue of Events in Rome* is a powerful example of the anticlerical literature that Erasmianism gave rise to in Spain, and in-deed so pervasive was the Erasmian spirit in these early years that when the papal nuncio requested the Inquisition to condemn the work, the Grand Inquisitor declared that to attack the morals of the pope and clergy did not in itself constitute heresy.

Philip II devoted many years to building the somberly magnificent Escorial as a fitting residence, monastery, and tomb for the Spanish Hapsburgs.

Although Charles forbade hostile criticism of Erasmus as late as 1527, this liberal attitude was not to last. Identification with the views of Luther made Erasmus and his followers suspect in Spain, and by 1547 Erasmus' works were to be found on the Spanish Index of prohibited books. The Inquisition was by now firmly in the control of the religious orders, and from this time on a series of Indexes was compiled to ensure that no material that in any way criticized the orders or challenged their authority was published. The persecution of the Protestant groups that had formed even in Spain now began in earnest. For the first, but by no means the last, time, Spain's liberal intellectuals were forced to choose exile or repression. Juan de Valdés and the famous Spanish educationalist, Luis Vives, had already left some years before. The chance for Spain to lead a free and open social and cultural life had been rejected, and the course was set for that claustrophobic, intolerant, and xenophobic existence which was to remain Spain's hallmark for centuries to come.

The religious question, of course, was by no means the only one that Charles had to face. His election to the imperial Crown placed under the rule of one nineteen-year-old youth Spain, the Indies and all that these were to entail, the Franche-Comté, Roussillon, the Low Countries, Germany, and half of Italy. It was the greatest and most powerful empire since Rome and could not but excite the envy, animosity, and suspicion of the two other major European powers, England and France. As effective head of this fabulous dominion, Spain bore the brunt of the endless and intricate wars that followed, never admittedly upon her own soil but at the severe cost of her economic well-being.

But it was not only from abroad that trouble came. At home, too, Charles' Spain was having serious teething trouble. No sooner had he left for Germany after his election to the Holy Roman Empire, nominating his former tutor Adrian of Utrecht as regent in his absence, than Castile, heart of the new empire, exploded into what is known as the Revolt of the Comuneros. Sparked by resentment of what was regarded as Charles' betrayal of Spain to foreign influence and interference, the rebellion graduated into a full-scale struggle for power between the Crown and the *comunidades,* or municipalities. City after city came out against the royal authority. A revolutionary *junta* was set up to put the cities' modest constitutional demands to

Charles, and attempts were even made by the rebels to proclaim poor mad Joanna queen. The regent's forces countered by setting fire to the great center of Spanish trade, Medina del Campo. The Battle of Villa-lar in 1521 put an end to the uprising when royalist forces defeated the *comunidades* and with them the Spanish middle class as an effective political power. The rebel leaders—Juan de Padilla, Juan Bravo, and Pedro Maldonado—were put to death, and the following year Charles made sure the message of Villalar had been taken to heart by marching his German troops through the leading recalcitrant cities.

The determination to brook no threat to the stability of the country or the authority of the Crown led Charles to pursue the policy of religious unification undertaken by Ferdinand and Isabella. The Va-lencian Moslems had not been included in Isabella's edict of 1502 offering either conversion or exile to those of the Moslem faith, but the hostility with which they were regarded by the mass of the common people was no different from that which had led to the imposition of this tragic measure in Castile. In 1525 Charles took the easiest, by now traditional, method of placating society by expelling from the kingdom of Aragon, including Valencia, all Moslems unwilling to accept bap-tism. The whole of Spain was now officially Christian, and Spain's obsession with the Christian ideal was becoming even more profound.

The violent burgeoning of the Protestant Reformation, anathema to the cult of orthodoxy established as national policy by Isabella, brought Spain right into the heart of the physical as well as spiritual struggle to which Martin Luther's teachings gave rise in northern Europe. Charles "owned" Germany and the Netherlands, and these were the very coun-tries in which local princes seized the opportunity of the religious schism to make a bid for independence and power. And since where Charles went Spain went too, she soon found herself cast in the leading role of defender of the Catholic conscience of Europe. Not only did she become the spokesman for Catholicism at the meetings of the Council of Trent—initially held in a little town in the Tyrol, at which the churchmen of Europe congregated to try to arrive at some working agreement between Rome and the new dissenters—but Spain also launched at this time a new religious order that was to help Rome com-bat the Protestant Reformation with a reformation of its own—the Counter-Reformation.

The story goes that in 1522 a wounded Basque soldier called Ignatius of Loyola received a heavenly sign while on a pilgrimage to the shrine of the Black Virgin, patron saint of Catalonia, in the mountains of Montserrat. The experience inspired him to envisage a new order of Christianity which would go forth to meet the world instead of withdrawing from it, a militant movement with a policy of aggressive proselytization which would profess absolute obedience to the pope. Accordingly in 1539 Ignatius of Loyola founded in Rome the Society of Jesus. Efficient, thorough, and ruthless, the Jesuit order has attracted more opprobrium from more quarters than any other religious organization. Even in the first half of the sixteenth century its creation pleased almost no one. The Inquisition and the other religious orders were immediately hostile to this threat to their influence; Loyola himself was interrogated twice by the Inquisition and forbidden to preach for three years. The Crown disapproved because of the Jesuit vow of complete obedience to Rome; for all her religious fervor Spain cherished the right to govern her own house, an attitude strengthened by the increasing conviction that Spain was more Catholic than the pope himself. However, for all the opposition, the Jesuits, as prime representatives of the church militant, took the van in the struggle against what they regarded as the Satanic forces of dissension. Within Spain they fomented an atmosphere of religious fervor and dedication which in the second half of the sixteenth century was to make Spain the major force behind the Counter-Reformation and lead to a truly remarkable body of original religious literature—of which the writings of the Spanish mystics form only the tip of the iceberg.

While Spain's sights at home and in Europe were becoming ever more narrowly focused, in another direction her horizons exploded to embrace a new hemisphere. On September 25, 1513, Vasco Núñez de Balboa, after crossing the Isthmus of Panama, became the first European to sight the Pacific Ocean. It was one of the most dramatic moments in history. When the news got back to Europe, the true significance of Columbus' earlier achievement struck home—in his search for a westerly route to the East he had discovered a continent. It was a continent, furthermore, not ruled by the fabled Prester John or some other powerful Eastern potentate, but apparently there, and easy, for the taking. With the Caribbean island of Hispaniola already under secure control, Spain had now acquired a foothold on the Pacific coast. And exploration of the new continent started in earnest as the excitement of the unknown added incentive to the dream of finding El Dorado. The era of the conquistadors had begun.

The conquest of Mexico, 1519–1522, by Hernán Cortés, and that of Peru by Francisco Pizarro between 1531 and 1535, together with their aftermath, are not episodes apart from the mainstream of Spanish history. On the contrary, the creation of an overseas Spanish Empire on the ruins of the conquered Aztec and Inca civilizations was inseparably involved with the unfolding of Spain's destiny back home. The Jesuits exported their missionary zeal to the vast and virgin territory across the Atlantic, to the increased displeasure of the Crown, which had pre-empted full ecclesiastical control in the new Spanish possessions. Spain herself, conqueror of Islam and defender of the Catholic faith, regarded it as her solemn duty to undertake the spiritual welfare of the conquered natives, ensuring that if they died they died Christians. A whole new world was ready to be won for God. The clash between these lofty and undoubtedly sincere aims and the material interests involved in the exploitation of the new empire was as bitter as it was inevitable and gave rise early on to fierce polemic within Spain. As the century wore on, interminable wars, a backward agriculture, and a foundering industry made imperative the taking of all the riches America could offer. Settlers had to be rewarded and mollified with grants of land and natives, and the central authority, trying to administer the new territories from a distance of some five thousand miles, was powerless to prevent abuse and control the greed of its subjects. The tragic brutality—main source of the "black legend" of Spain—with which conquest and settlement were carried out has cast a terrible shadow upon the undoubted fortitude and heroism of the handful of Castilians, Andalusians, and Extremadurans responsible for the conquests. Marching into the unknown they survived conditions almost unbearable to man and against overwhelming odds wrenched a continent away from its native inhabitants.

The supreme irony lies in the fact that it is possible to regard the acquisition and colonization of America as, not the saving, but the downfall of Spain. In the first place, whatever the realities, its overseas empire bequeathed upon Spain an aura of wealth and power that drew toward it the hostile guns and covetous eyes of Europe. This had not only political but very basic material consequences. Cortés' first consignment of Aztec treasure was snatched in transit by the king of France and the outrage proved to be but a foretaste of things to come. Spanish bullion on its way across the Atlantic became fair game for any buccaneer eager to win the favor of his outwardly innocent sovereign. It was a game played later on with great relish by Elizabeth of England and her sea captains, Walter Raleigh, John Hawkins, and Francis Drake, and one which the Dutch too were not slow in learning. In spite of the piracy the treasure that did reach Seville, Castile's home port for the New World fleet, was considerable. But it did not for long remain in the Torre del Oro, the Golden Tower, on the waterfront of the Guadalquivir where bullion was counted and registered. Most of it poured into the coffers of German and Italian bankers to finance Charles' religious and political wars in Europe; even so, there was nowhere near enough for the purpose.

But most debilitating of all was the way in which American gold and silver—the famous silver mountain, Potosí, was discovered in 1545—

A view of the primitive silver refinery at Potosí, in Bolivia, 1584

came to be regarded as the panacea for all Spain's financial ills. On many occasions the timely arrival of a new shipment averted a crisis, but an unreliable flow of treasure was no adequate substitute for a solid, prosperous economy, as Spain was soon to learn. Blinded by the glitter, Spain failed to use her new riches to stimulate her own economic growth, and later when the influx of bullion became a trickle she would be left with nothing. There were in addition very positive immediate disadvantages: the flood of precious metals created an inflationary spiral in Europe, and particularly in Spain, with which Spain's unstable economy was unable to cope. Between 1520 and 1550 prices doubled (they were to double again by the end of that century) and foreign trade suffered as a result. Industry foundered and, in the interest of a soaring wool trade whose prosperity was not, alas, to last, agriculture was further sacrificed to the demands of the Mesta.

An answer to Spain's financial problems was increasingly sought in rocketing taxes, the main burden of which, owing to the tax exemptions enjoyed by nobles, military orders, and the Church, was borne by those least able to pay. Finally, but by no means least important, America was to prove a terrible drain on Spain's human resources. The men who flocked there eager for the promises of a new land could not be replaced. The wars in Europe and the attractions of a celibate religious life that offered both security and authority further reduced the able-bodied working population. With the promise of easy wealth overseas and of military booty in Europe, with the traditional association of industry and commerce with Moslems and Jews, with the growing role played in Spain's economy by foreigners, work became an unattractive, un-Spanish, and un-Christian concept, to be avoided at all costs. Rather than earn his living by honest labor, Quevedo's Pablos in *La vida del Buscón* (1626) preferred to starve and sprinkle his clothes with crumbs so that the world might think he had eaten. He provides a splendid literary symbol of that aversion to work and contempt and distaste for industry which was to have such disastrous consequences for the Spanish economy.

On the accession of Charles in 1517 the future had seemed set fair for Spain. By 1529, the year in which Charles taunted his rivals with his magnificently lavish coronation as Holy Roman Emperor in Bologna, Spain's sacrifice to the ambitions of her monarch was well under-

soon began to put the first nails in the coffin. What successes there
were, were only partial. Two and a half decades of war with a France
frustrated in its own imperial vision and wary of encirclement by Spain
yielded glorious moments for Charles—amongst them the brilliant victory at Pavia in 1525 during the struggle for Milan, when the French
king himself, Francis I, was taken prisoner. Nine years later, with
Milan still at issue, Charles, like one of the knights in his favorite
chivalresque novels, challenged his enemy to personal combat. This
offer to solve the question at one stroke was, however, turned down.
France had shaken itself freer of the Middle Ages than had Spain.

Although they brought minor gains, the French wars did not
substantially alter the power structure of Europe. France remained a
powerful and essentially hostile neighbor. In the Mediterranean, meanwhile, Charles had undertaken the protection of Europe and Christianity from the swiftly advancing Ottoman Turks. Again there were successes—Charles personally led an attack on Turkish-occupied Tunis in
1535 and succeeded in capturing the city and freeing thousands of
Christian slaves. But the advance of the Turks was not halted. As for
the religious contest, nothing could stem its irreversible course. The
moderating influence of Luther died with him in 1546 and the rise of
Calvinism made the Protestants as dogmatic and unyielding as Rome
itself. When the pope declared a holy war against the Protestant princes
of Germany, Charles led his Spanish and Flemish troops to the defense
of his faith and his empire. In 1547 he won the Battle of Mühlberg
only to be decisively defeated five years later at Innsbruck. The Council
of Trent failed to arrive at any compromise, and in 1555 the Diet of
Augsburg proclaimed the right of every German prince to determine
the religion of his own state. Germany had become the leader of the
Reformation and Charles had failed as defender of the Holy Roman
Empire. But Spain had not learned that it is impossible to win ideo-
logical battles with physical force.

In 1556 Charles acknowledged his defeat by abdicating the thrones
of Spain, Italy, and the Netherlands in favor of his son Philip; the
German Empire he passed to his brother Ferdinand. Then, after spend-
ing twenty of his forty years in power away from Spain, he returned
there for the first time in thirteen years, to prepare for death. With his

parrot and his cat he retired to the monastery of Yuste in Extremadura. Almost toothless and plagued with gout he settled down to enjoy his garden and the watches and clocks he took pleasure in repairing. His glutton's appetite he indulged, to the despair of his retainers, until he could no longer lift a finger, so crippling was his gout. But his thoughts lingered constantly on death and a few months after his withdrawal from the world he insisted on attending a rehearsal of his own funeral. After the Requiem Mass he retreated to his garden. Here, that creeping, chilling wind of the central plateau which in Castilian lore can kill a man without extinguishing a flame, finally achieved what continuous wars and physical hardship had failed to do. The erstwhile emperor caught a cold that developed into a fever, and shortly afterward he died with his wife's crucifix in his hands and the name of Jesus on his stiffening lips. He was fifty-five years old.

Before Charles had left Brussels, his former seat, for Spain, he had summoned to that city his son Philip. In a brilliant and emotion-charged scene of farewell in the palace of the dukes of Brabant, the emperor bequeathed to Philip his mighty heritage, enjoining him "to be a strenuous defender of the Catholic faith, and of law and justice which are the bulwarks of Empire." The role of defender of the faith was one which Philip was to occupy with even more fervor than his father. Philip's declaration that he "would rather not rule than rule over heretics" explains a great deal in Spanish policy at home and abroad during his reign and that of many who came after.

His father's legacy brought with it strains which the divestment

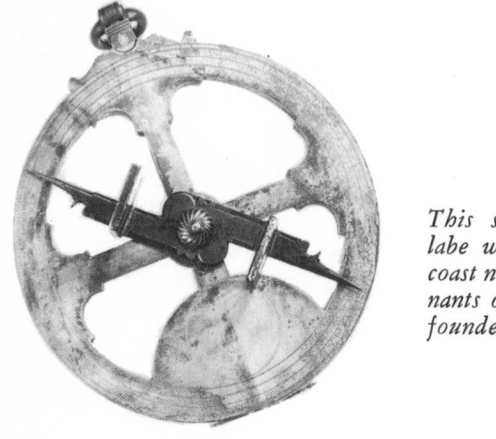

This sixteenth-century astrolabe was found on the Irish coast near the spot where remnants of the Spanish Armada foundered en route home.

of the Holy Roman Empire added to rather than diminished. With Germany gone, the Netherlands could only be maintained and defended from the sea alone, an uneasy situation depending as it did upon the cooperation or subjugation of France and England. And Spain's acquisition of Milan and Naples ensured the hostility of France, which continued to entertain its ambitions in the direction of Italy in spite of formally renouncing its claim to Milan, in exchange for the return of some two hundred towns and villages on the Franco-Spanish border. As far as England was concerned, Philip's reign (1556–1598) was the period in which Spain and England danced their elaborate menacing galliard of flirtation and deadly rivalry. England's religious schism was one in which Spain felt particularly involved—in embracing Protestantism with Anne Boleyn, Henry VIII had spurned not only Rome but Catherine of Aragon and Spain. And the fact that Catherine's daughter, Mary Tudor, was second in line to the English throne had done much to keep Spain's interest in that direction alive, adding a good measure of political enthusiasm to religious zeal. It was in an attempt to secure the Netherlands and alter the balance of power with France in his favor, that Charles had negotiated the marriage of Philip to the English Catholic princess in 1554. His plans were spoiled not long after by Mary's childless death, but Spain continued to flirt with England when Mary's resolutely English and resolutely Protestant sister, Elizabeth, had succeeded to the throne. Philip even went as far as asking her, too, to become his bride—religious scruples could be sacrificed to the greater good of Catholic Europe. It was in accord with this firm belief that upon the supremacy and power of Spain depended the future of Catholicism, that Philip saw fit to support Elizabeth against Mary Queen of Scots, who had dangerous connections with France.

Just as his policies abroad were dictated by His Most Catholic Majesty's almost fanatical sense of religious mission, so too at home. Determined to avoid contagion with a Europe riddled with heterodoxy, Spain during this period turned in upon itself, resolutely closing its doors to the outside world. Many of Spain's intellectuals during the previous reign had succeeded in arriving at a compromise between the claims of orthodoxy and the exciting new horizons offered them by the Renaissance. The Renaissance, of course, continued to exert its influence but in no way which conflicted with strict Catholic dogma. Any step taken out of line and the inquisitorial watchdog pounced. Even the Church itself was not immune. In 1559 the very head of the Spanish Church, the archbishop of Toledo, was arrested and subjected to an investigation that dragged on for seventeen years. Jealousy and rivalry between the various religious orders made an ugly situation uglier still and led to the arrest, or at least the investigation, of noted religious writers like Fray Luis de León and the mystics Saint Teresa and Saint John of the Cross. In these cases and many others, the victims' innocence was eventually established, but often not until after years of deprivation.

Spanish culture then and afterward inevitably suffered from this enforced cloistering of the Spanish intellectual and creative genius—the publication and import of books were rigidly controlled and Spaniards were prohibited from studying in foreign universities other than Bologna. New developments in learning and in empirical science were denied Spain and at this point her backwardness in education and research was born. In the reign of Philip's grandson, Philip IV, a committee of the theologians passed the following judgment on a plan to canalize the Manzanares and the Tagus rivers: "If God had wanted these two rivers to be navigable he could have effected it simply by a 'fiat,' and it would be an infringement of the rights of Providence to improve that which, for reason's not to be understood, it had wished to remain unperfect."

And yet out of Counter-Reformation Spain came a remarkable literature, a literature shaped directly or indirectly by the religious spirit of the age which nevertheless rises above and beyond it. The religious upheaval in Europe that led to the breakup of the Renaissance world and its dream of human perfection, created in Spain a new literary realism —largely satirical in tone and moralistic in emphasis—that set itself the task of exploring the psychological realities and social tensions of life instead of escaping from them into an idealized existence where evil, cruelty, and ugliness did not enter. The fact that Lope de Vega took holy orders, that Tirso de Molina was a Mercedarian friar, that Góngora took deacon's orders, that Calderón became a priest and Gracián a Jesuit, by no means cut them off from the world and did not stop them from writing movingly and perceptively about the tragicomedy of man's life. Cervantes' *Don Quijote* (1605), coming as it does at the meeting of two very different centuries, reflects that tension

between illusion and reality, between idealism and empiricism, between hope and despair, that was the outcome at the time of the conflict between past aspirations and growing pessimism. It was a conflict
inevitable throughout Europe after the high-water mark of optimism
of the Renaissance, but in Spain it was a conflict made much more painful by a dawning realization of the political, social, and economic realities of Spain's situation. Toward the end of Philip II's reign, the her-
mit historian Juan de Mariana could warn that Spain was tottering
beneath its own weight, and intellectuals began to curse the day when
Spain had offended Heaven by confusing the elements of earth and
water and crossing the "Ocean Sea."

Spain's withdrawal into itself after the accession of Philip II was
reflected appropriately enough in the behavior of the monarch himself. Charles had been an active leader, marching at the head of his
armies and traveling relentlessly among his possessions. His son was
a ruler of a very different order. After a few early excursions, Philip
returned to the Peninsula in 1559 and never set foot outside it again.
He made Madrid—as yet historically unimportant but geographically
central—his fixed capital for administrative purposes, and two years
later began to build, some thirty miles to the northwest, the somber
monastery-palace of the Escorial as a tomb for his father and a retreat
for himself. Seated at his desk, first in the alcazar in Madrid and twenty
years later in the Escorial itself, Philip the Prudent, Europe's first bureaucratic king, manipulated the reigns of his farflung empire.

The process of centralization initiated by Charles was completed,
and a vast civil service burgeoned to cope with the delegation of responsibility that was the inevitable outcome. Even so, everything eventually reached Philip himself, setting out again subsequently from this
central point of omnipotence to the very tips of the administrative fingers. The machinery of state ground slower and slower as the years
went by, and bureaucratic efficiency disappeared under a mountain of
paper and red tape. The delay that accompanied the Crown's every
move created at this point the legend of the Spanish *"mañana"* —"If
death came from Spain," the viceroy of Naples caustically commented,
"we should live a long time." To his enemies at home and abroad during and long after his reign, Philip seemed like some huge, malevolent
spider, immobile at the center of his web yet fully sensitive—through

a reputedly vast army of spies—to everything that went on within his world-wide orbit.

So strongly identified did he become with that instrument of his religious policy, the Inquisition, that the image of the fanatical, tyrannical monster for centuries obscured the dutiful son, the devoted husband, the affectionate father, and the kind master. He was—by autocratic standards—truthful; he was frugal, generous, and dedicated to the pursuit of justice, as well as bigoted. Certainly Philip exacted no standards that he did not meet himself and for all his power—"at the slightest movement of that nation the whole earth trembled," said a proud Spanish historian—his court was the most austere in Europe.

With Philip, Spain entered a period of predominantly religious wars. France, the main enemy, and Italy, the main battle arena during the previous reign, occupied little of his attention, though France continued to lurk, bristling with contained hostility, in the wings. The storm broke in the 1560s. The rise of Calvinism and the religious wars it provoked in France from 1562 on, alerted Catholic Spain and her Catholic master to the full dangers of the Protestant threat. With heresy looming close, Spain prepared to dig in her heels. But if the mother country herself was not to be seriously contaminated, the Low Countries were a very different matter. From the early 1560s religious dissent and political unrest spread like wildfire there, and in August, 1566, Calvinist mobs rioted and sacked the churches. Philip found himself faced with a twofold rebellion against all that Spain stood for—terrestrial hegemony and spiritual orthodoxy. At the instigation of the duke of Alba, Philip opted for a policy of military action which would he hoped be brief and decisive. And the duke of Alba himself was dispatched to the Netherlands with an army to subdue the revolt. The battle with Protestantism had begun.

Cut off from the Netherlands as Spain was, the Catholic struggle for supremacy quickly acquired a maritime flavor, and at sea Spain was still weak. The English raided Spanish bullion ships from the Caribbean and Breton seamen harassed Spanish shipping in the Gulf of Gascony. In the winter of 1568–69 communications with the Netherlands were for a time completely cut off. Heresy seemed to be engulfing Europe. But the religious threat was not only a Protestant one. In the Mediterranean the standard of the crescent moon of Islam was fast

The piety of Catholic Spain is evident in this 1639 painting by Zurbarán.

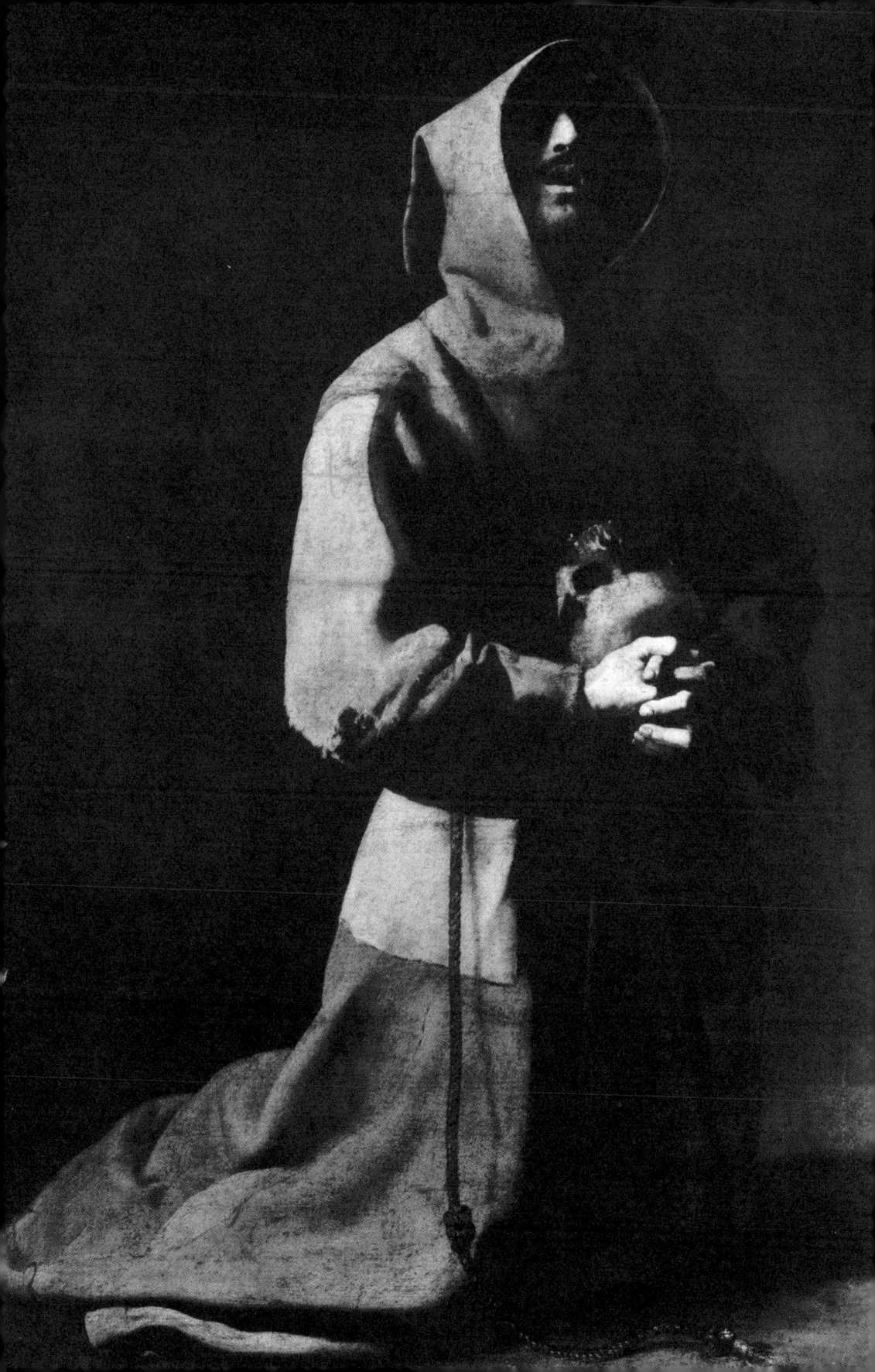

obliterating that of the Cross and reawakening the buried hopes and longings of Spain's Moriscos. On Christmas night in 1568—the fatal year of broken communication with the Netherlands, of the death of Philip's beloved third wife, Elizabeth of Valois, and of the unavoidable arrest and subsequent natural death of his vicious, intriguing son, Don Carlos—further calamity struck the long-suffering monarch. Morisco outlaws brought news to the city of Granada that a Morisco revolt—born of the severe repression suffered by the former Moslems of Andalusia—had broken out in the Alpujarras. The specter of vanished Islam had come back to haunt Spain's Most Catholic King.

The omens of gloom were gathering, but in spite of the Catholic struggle, in spite of the increasing burden of taxation and the foundering industry—which together let loose an ever-growing flood of vagrants and beggars upon the Spanish towns and countryside—Philip's reign had its moments of euphoria, and superficially at least Spain seemed to be holding its own. The Moriscos of the south were dispersed by proclamation throughout Castile, and the immediate danger from Granada thus removed. After years of naval impasse in the Mediterranean, a combined Christian force of over 200 galleys and 28,000 men under the leadership of Philip's half brother, the handsome, gifted Don John of Austria, achieved a spectacular victory over the Turks at Lepanto (the Greek Návpaktos) in 1571. The triumph did not seriously affect the Ottoman issue in any lasting way, but it was regarded by an elated Europe as a divine deliverance, while Spain acquired in Don John another great crusading hero.

In 1580 Philip even realized, after almost a thousand years, the Castilian dream of peninsular unity by successfully claiming accession to the throne of Portugal. King Sebastian of Portugal had died in 1578 at the Battle of Alcazarquivir, in the calamitous rout of a Portuguese fleet and army that had set out from Lisbon to bring the emperor of Morocco to his knees. In a four-hour battle in the scorching desert, the king, most of his nobles, and 8,000 men were destroyed and 15,000 taken captive. Europe was stunned and so too was Spain. But the shock did not prevent Philip from realizing that with the succession unsecured, he, as nephew and son-in-law of Sebastian's father, had a major claim. This he reinforced in 1580 with a Spanish army sent into Portugal, and in December of that year he himself arrived in Lisbon to become Portugal's new king. The new unity was threatened in the 1590s, when Aragon, after years of angry rumblings, revolted in defense of ancient privileges, but the Castilian army again came to the rescue.

In the Netherlands, meanwhile, revolt after revolt was put down in a series of campaigns noted for their brutality and destined eventually, by the very nature of the struggle, to failure. The launching in 1567 of the duke of Alba's campaign of terror during which five hundred people were sentenced to death on a single day rendered the reimposition of Spanish authority forever impossible. In 1576 the insult to Flemish pride came with the "day of the Spanish fury," when Philip's unpaid troops turned snarling on what appeared the source of their woes and attacked the city of Antwerp. The hero of Lepanto, Don John of Austria, was sent to save the day, but before the Netherlands would even recognize him as governor he was forced to agree reluctantly to the removal of all Spanish troops. The withdrawal was short-lived for, taking the law in his own hands, Don John called the Spanish forces back to fight on Flemish soil. In spite of his efforts, when he died in 1578 only two Flemish provinces remained under Spanish control.

Although the Netherlands was a constant drain on Spanish energies and resources, Philip's failure to pacify it does not seem to have scratched the surface of Spanish complacency in any serious way. The first real setback, when it came, was administered from elsewhere, from England. Don John had consented to go to the Netherlands largely because he regarded it as an ideal launching pad for an invasion of England—his ambition was to conquer England for Catholicism and for himself, and marry Mary Queen of Scots. But although Philip was not ready then for war with Elizabeth, war eventually did come. From 1583 on, the invasion of the island realm was presented to the king as an enterprise which could be carried out economically, which would wreak a glorious revenge for Catholicism, and which would enable Spain at last to reduce the Netherlands once and for all. Philip's acquiescence—precipitated partly by English intervention in the Netherlands—resulted in the first really crushing blow dealt Spain since the first flowering of her imperial ambitions: the defeat of the so-called Invincible Armada in 1588. The era of euphoria had ended.

The shock to the Spanish system was so shattering because the hopes, the confidence, and the religious zeal invested in the expedition had been so great. Priests had denounced the wicked heretic English and their unlawful queen from their pulpits and the Jesuit Pedro de Ribadeneira, in a rousing address to the men who were to go on the expedition, had stated, "I consider this enterprise the most important undertaking by God's Church for many hundreds of year." The Armada was to be the avenging arm of God, castigating the perpetrators of the Great Schism and fulfilling Spain's divine destiny. The only flaw in the great design was that the Armada was not invincible. The duke of Medina-Sidonia, appointed its commander against his will, knew it, and Philip suspected it, but the Spanish army had somehow to be transported to the English shores. From the outset the venture seemed doomed. The departure was delayed a year by Drake's raids on Lisbon and Cádiz, and when the Armada did eventually set sail from Lisbon it got no farther than La Coruña on the northwest tip of Spain before it had to put in to port for repairs. When it reached the English Channel, this force of 130 ships and 30,000 underfed scurvy-ridden men was met by battering storms and an English fleet that was better equipped, more skillfully manned, and more competently led. Like terriers snapping at the throat of a sick bull, English ships ran rings round the lurching Spanish galleons, many of which were barely seaworthy. The end was never in doubt. And although one half of the Spanish fleet managed to limp home in ignominy to form the basis of a new and stronger sea force, England remained inviolate, Spain was humiliated in the eyes of the world, and Spanish morale had been irreparably wounded. And with reason. The defeat of the Armada was the great turning point in Spain's fortunes, for although the future still held its successes, the Netherlands would not now be pacified, France would become once more a great power, and Portugal would eventually be lost.

In Germany, England, and the Lowlands Philip's self-appointed mission to preserve intact the Catholic faith had failed. The one consolation was that in France, nearest to Spain, his stern watchfulness was instrumental, albeit in a rather roundabout way, in preventing France as a nation from embracing the Protestant faith. The irony was that Philip witnessed his faith triumph there at the cost of his own political ambitions. After the assassination of the childless French king, Henry III, Philip expected that he as brother-in-law, or his daughter Isabella as niece, might inherit the French Crown. His rival was the

Protestant Henry of Navarre, and the French people themselves were severely torn by the complicated challenge to their allegiance. Spanish troops entered the country ready to enforce Philip's claim. In 1593, however, Henry solved the problem by sacrificing religious conscience to political success and turning Catholic. France went to Navarre; Spain had been flouted yet again.

From his bare gloomy office in the Escorial, Philip had watched Spain come to grief on the twin reefs of religious dissension and national pride. But the scene within Castile was even more disheartening. Such was Spain's inability to adapt herself to the emerging capitalist world, to grasp the essential requirements for a sound economy, that even when her political, military, and colonial fortunes had been in the ascent her internal affairs were firmly established on the slippery slope toward disaster. The rich sank their money into what was safe, tangible, and lasting—palaces, churches, monasteries, sculpture, and painting, instead of into trade, agriculture, and industry. Famine, disease, taxes, enclosures, and the gradual paralyzation of industry had slowly brought the people to their knees. In 1596 Castile was declared bankrupt for the third time in one reign, and in that very same year

On December 31, 1585, Drake's fleet massed ominously in the harbor before a raid on Santo Domingo, a Spanish colony on Hispaniola.

Sir Francis Drake sacked the rich but helpless port of Cádiz for the second time, sinking every vessel in the harbor. As Philip, now a sick man, waited for death to claim him, what did he think of the rewards that his piety and his relentless determination to save Europe for God and the pope had brought Spain and his people? Thanks to him the floodgates against the Protestant tide had held in France and Spain, but on the other side of the gates the waters would not now retreat.

That his awareness of what Flanders had meant for Spain was both acute and distressing is certain. For in his will he separated them, leaving that part of the Netherlands still subject to Castile to his daughter Isabella and her husband, Archduke Albert of Austria. But even now he could not rid himself of paternalistic concern for the true faith, and he not only stipulated that Flanders should return to Spain should his daughter die without an heir, but also arranged for Spanish garrisons to remain on Flemish soil—to ensure that the continuing specter of Spanish might would keep the Flemish in their place. The running sore thus continued to run. All in all, his legacy was not a happy one. When he died in 1598, "withered and feeble" after a long and painful illness through which never a word of self-pity or complaint is said to have escaped his lips, he left Spain an empty treasury and a son who was weak and inexperienced—inexperienced because Philip II could tolerate no other man but himself in control of his empire's affairs. An extremely able man, hard, grim, and dedicated, Philip, and Spain with him, was the victim of qualities in himself that are normally adjudged to be virtues in less powerful spheres of life—piety and conscientiousness. These qualities made him ultimately a failure, removing him as they did from the economic, administrative, and psychological realities of the modern world. On his deathbed he must have realized at last that even the king of Spain could not prevail against poverty, hardship, and exhaustion at home, or the conscience of men at large.

The century that began with the accession of Philip III, the feeble son of Philip II's marriage to his niece Anne of Austria, was a century of poignant contrast. For this period of unsurpassed literary brilliance was also the age when the cancer of Spain's ills rose to the surface and proceeded to devour the visible as well as the hidden body of Spain. The colossus of the sixteenth century—great for the expanse of its vision as well as for the extent of its territories—suffered a process of severe political, social, and economic decline which culminated in the reign of Charles II with a total loss of prestige.

The deterioration was all-embracing, and was symbolized at the very top in the persons of the Hapsburg monarchs themselves. Philip III (*r.* 1598–1621) and his son Philip IV (*r.* 1621–1665) were but shadows of their great ancestors and recognized the fact by handing over the reins of government to their favorites, the duke of Lerma and the count-duke of Olivares respectively. Charles II (*r.* 1665–1700) was a crazed impotent, entirely unfit to rule, and the victim throughout his life of court intrigue. The vigor and zeal of the Catholic Monarchs, inherited by Charles V and Philip II, had played itself out and disintegrated into apathy and incompetence. The degeneration was reflected in court life and throughout society as a whole. At court the mood of gravity imposed by Philip II yielded to one of frivolity and extravagance that percolated down to other levels of society, particularly in the capital. Philip III and his ministers squandered their time in the hunt, the theater, and lavish court *fiestas.* Laws aimed at curbing expenditure—by limiting the amount of material in a dress or ruff and the number of horses that pulled the carriages of the rich—were passed and ignored. So too were laws intended to improve public morals: carriages were not to be used with the curtains closed and near relatives were the only male companions allowed to accompany a woman when she rode in one. Courtesans and prostitutes were forbidden to ride in carriages at all. But to no effect.

The encroachment upon public life of what the Spaniards appropriately call public women is one of the most remarkable features of this time. Respectable women were forced into seclusion as they shunned those pursuits that their less virtuous sisters had usurped. By the middle of the century there were eight hundred all-night brothels in Madrid alone. In the reign of Philip IV the morals of the capital and the court, which was lavish and ostentatious to a degree that would have made the king's grandfather blench, never failed to elicit the disapproval of shocked foreigners. And the ripples of scandal touched the very great. In 1641 three *grandees* were banished for scaling the walls of the royal palace, the Retiro, at night and making love to some maids of honor, while shortly before that the surface of social respectability had been violently agitated by the revelation of a series of liaisons

between aristocratic women of the highest eminence and their male servants. Philip IV himself was a libertine tormented by crises of guilt that drove him to establish an extraordinary relationship with a nun, Sor María de Agreda, to whom he confessed his faults in a series of letters. The correspondence did not prevent the king from fathering upon his various mistresses at least thirty illegitimate children.

The decline in social standards was a reflection of a grave national malaise. The delegation of government to two grandees marks the political supremacy of the landed aristocrats, and under the duke of Lerma, administrative and bureaucratic corruption reached heights unknown since Isabella had initiated her policy of appointments through merit. Public offices and honors now went to those who could pay for them. The ravages of war, famine, pestilence, and poverty emptied cities and countryside. In 1669 a Spanish minister reported: "I visit many places which a few years ago contained a thousand households and now contain only five hundred; and some of the five hundred scarcely show signs of having a hundred; and in all of them there are innumerable people and families who go for a day or two without breaking their fast, and others who simply eat grasses they collect in the countryside, and other means of sustenance never before used."

Agriculture foundered, looms fell silent. At the beginning of the century the currency was devalued and thereafter financial crisis followed financial crisis until the great economic collapse of the country in 1680. Peace had been concluded with France, the Netherlands, and England in the early years, but the opportunity to set the Spanish house in order was passed by. The way in which the duke of Lerma coped with hostile criticism in 1601 gives the flavor of the age: he petulantly persuaded Philip to move his capital to Valladolid. Five years later a ruined Madrid bribed Philip III into moving his court back again and Lerma received a palace for facilitating the deal.

The Spanish people, meanwhile, escaped the grim realities of life by despising the material world that was denied them and embracing vaguer but less painful prizes—religion, honor, purity of blood, and nobility: if they could not uncover coats of arms on their family trees, then they bought them. The church, the bullfight, the auto-da-fé, the theater, the religious feast, for a while relieved and colored a sense of pessimism and a pressure of day-to-day existence that were difficult to

The strict social conventions of seventeenth-century Spain are captured in this portrait of a wistful young girl and her ever-vigilant dueña, *by Murillo.*

bear. In the articulate, pessimism became black despair and cynicism, as the seemingly irremediable ills of society cast a shadow on the very nature of Man himself. The satiricist Quevedo remarked, "Treat women as you treat everything else—use them but don't trust them." But the cold, considered judgment of the Jesuit Gracián in his allegorical novel *El Criticón* (1657) was, "As long as there are men, there is no need to attribute all the evil in the world to women." For the seventeenth century so much of life was false—female beauty, material well-being, happiness, the beauty of a flower, even the blueness of God's sky— that the only wisdom was *desengaño*: disillusionment. The child as soon as it was born began the long descent toward death, and the one true reality was the spiritual one, the one true life the life after death. For Calderón, mouthpiece of seventeenth-century Catholic Spain, "The whole of life is a dream, and dreams themselves are but dreams."

Although the divide between the two centuries was in many ways very great there was no real break in governmental policy—the old attitudes and allegiances, and the wrong decisions to which they led,

A Flemish engraving shows a Spanish drummer, fifer, and halberdier.

continued as before. One of the most disastrous pieces of legislation was the final step in Spain's long fight for religious supremacy and unity within her shores. The Moriscos represented Spain's major agricultural labor force. They were hard-working and, since they married early and sent none of their children to swell the growing ranks of religious celibates, they were prolific. (In 1626 there were nine thousand religious houses for men in Castile alone.) Spain could ill afford to lose such qualities. Yet, from 1609 onward, Spain, with a population of roughly only nine million, expelled from its shores between three and five hundred thousand Moriscos because she had been unable to assimilate them satisfactorily and feared the resulting threat of their continuing contact with the Moslem world outside. And she did it with hardly a thought for making good their loss to the Spanish countryside and the economy at large. The country lost a major source of energy, while the injustice to the victims—Spaniards of centuries' standing—does not bear thinking about.

As far as military commitment abroad was concerned, Spain continued to behave like a great power and the peace treaties with France, England, and the Netherlands did for a short time revitalize her waning prestige. An unlikely ally was found for a declaration of war on Turkey: the shah of Persia. But Spain's naval strength had almost vanished and little headway was made. War broke out in Italy again in 1615 and limped on for some years. Spain's major military engagement in the seventeenth century, however, took place on that stage of former Spanish failure—Germany, where hostilities broke out between the Protestant north and the Catholic south and eventually dragged Europe into the maelstrom of the Thirty Years' War.

When Philip IV—young and pleasure-loving—came to the throne in 1621, his appointed minister, the energetic and hugely ambitious count-duke of Olivares, terrorized the councils of Spain into accepting a fully autocratic regime and forced centralization upon the country's autonomous regions, Portugal and Catalonia. He then led Spain into the Thirty Years' War, thereby neglecting the defense of Spain's interests in America, and, when France under Richelieu intervened in the war, Olivares brought down upon Spain animosities that were to prove disastrously costly. In 1639 the treasure fleet failed to cross the Atlantic at all. In that year too, Catalonia, driven to extremes by

OVERLEAF: *The Battle of Lepanto, 1571, was a stunning victory for a combined Spanish and Italian fleet, seen in the foreground clashing with Turkish galleys.*

Madrid's arrogant and unconstitutional exploitation, and encouraged by a now hostile France, erupted into armed revolt. In 1640 on Corpus Christi Day, the Corpus of Blood as it is known, the rebels who had passed from town to town, killing, burning, and intimidating, swept into Barcelona, terrorized and killed all the representatives of the Castilian government they could find, set fire to houses, books, and papers, and stabbed to death the Castilian viceroy, the corpulent count of Santa Coloma, as he lay on the beach fainting with the pain from an ankle he had broken while trying to escape. Six months later, Portugal too took her fate once again into her own hands, overthrew the central authority in Lisbon, and acclaimed the duke of Braganza king.

In 1642 Olivares was dismissed. But it was too late to save more than the shreds of Castilian dignity. Upon the battlefields of Europe the formerly glorious Spanish infantry left their flags and their reputation in tatters—at the battles of Rocroi (1643), Lens (1648), and the Dunes (1658). In 1653 Catalonia obtained recognition of her special liberties, and in 1668 Portugal consolidated her independence forever.

The reign of Charles II—called the Bewitched in an attempt to excuse his terrible inadequacies—is a painful epilogue to a tragic story. Physically malformed and mentally subnormal, he could not sit unsupported until the age of six, and he never managed to learn to eat or speak properly. He succeeded to the throne in 1665 at the age of four, and survived as nominal head of the dying Spanish Empire for thirty-five years. Spain needed a savior, and received instead a retarded wretch incapable of governing or producing an heir. For thirty-five years he was the center of endless intrigue at home, and international conspiracy abroad; on his death Europe went to war to decide who should have Spain. The Hapsburg legacy had ruined Spain, and its last Spanish son, "stunted sprig of a degenerate line," placed it at the mercy of the world.

The period is a dark and confused one. Until Charles came of age at fifteen, his mother Mariana acted as regent, scheming on behalf of Austria and delegating government to favorites whom she foisted on the country against the will of the people. Her bitterest enemy was Charles' illegitimate half brother, son of Philip IV and a Madrid actress, called, like a previous royal bastard, Don John of Austria. Like his famous predecessor he was a virile and able man, thirty-five years old when the infant Charles succeeded to the throne. Eventually successful in ousting Mariana from power, he reigned for a time supreme. But in 1679 he mysteriously died and ten years later, Mariana, whispered to be his murderer, herself was found dead, again from no obvious cause.

Throughout the reign feeble Spain battled with France, whose ambitious and scheming Louis XIV leaped at the opportunity to attack the possessions of the moribund giant. The betrothal of the king with Louis' unhappy niece, Marie-Louise of Orléans, did nothing to help the situation. In Flanders and in Catalonia Spain was driven to try to defend her territory. But in spite of help from other countries—England, Sweden, the empire, Holland—who gave support as the balance of power swung in Spain's favor, and in spite of the unswerving and undeserved loyalty of the Catalans who for some inexplicable reason felt a deep sense of loyalty to their ailing king, Spain barely held her own. Artois, the Franche-Comté, and the great frontier towns of Flanders were lost. After thirty years of war, peace came at last in 1697, but not for long. As Charles' pathetic body and mind weakened, France and the Austrian Empire intrigued in favor of their claims to the Spanish throne and to enlist the support of Europe for their plans. Both Louis XIV and Emperor Leopold were grandsons of Philip III and both had married daughters of Philip IV. Charles himself, after the death of his French wife, had been made to marry an Austrian. So the claims were about equal. The choice, when it came, proved a triumph for the French faction. In October, 1700, Charles, making nonsense of all Spain's military struggles of the preceding thirty years, decided in favor of Philip of Anjou, second son of the French dauphin. He died before he could be persuaded to change his mind. But Austria did not take the outcome lying down and barely before the new king had replaced the old, the War of the Spanish Succession had erupted. Spain, for the first but not the last time, had become Europe's pawn.

CHAPTER VI

ENLIGHTENMENT
AND TRADITION

The period that followed upon the age of the Spanish Hapsburgs was very different in flavor from the defeated, pessimistic, claustrophobic, and religion-haunted century of Spain's decline. During the eighteenth century hope and enthusiasm stirred once again in Spanish breasts. The new Bourbon dynasty, which succeeded the Hapsburgs, signaled for many Spain's re-entry into Europe after a century of cloistered hostility; and Europe in the eighteenth century means the Enlightenment. There were to be "no more Pyrenees."

The hope and enthusiasm were to a large extent justified. With the arrival of Philip V (*r.* 1700–1746), at the very dawn of the new century, a program of reform was initiated; its pace would accelerate as the years went by, culminating in the second half of the century in the reign of that extremely able and highly enlightened despot Charles III. Under these kings of French descent, Spain regained some of her former confidence and vitality and for a time, the last time, took on again the semblance of a great power.

The face of Spain itself was considerably affected by the complete

In "Ash Wednesday," Goya satirizes peasant festivals, suggesting an underlying savagery in this pre-Lenten revel.

change of rule. The War of the Spanish Succession (1701–1714) gave the new dynasty the chance to put into effect that aspect of its reforming policy which it regarded as paramount—centralization. For Spain was as divided as the rest of Europe over the terms of Charles the Bewitched's will. While Castile staunchly supported the French claim, Aragon and Catalonia could not resist the opportunity of striking a blow against the central authority in Madrid. Barcelona accordingly became the headquarters of Archduke Charles of Austria when he established a government to rival that in Madrid, and in 1706 the archduke was proclaimed king of Aragon. Ferdinand and Isabella's work seemed in danger of being permanently undone. But five years later the archduke also became emperor of Austria and this proved too much for England, up until now an ally of the Austro-Catalan faction. England changed sides, and finally in 1714 Barcelona surrendered to the troops of Philip V, leaving Aragon wide open, a rebellious region rendered totally vulnerable by defeat. The opportunity to deal effectively with Spanish separatism had come at last.

Philip set about molding Castile and Aragon into a true nation. The Cortes of Aragon was merged into that of Castile, and Aragon was given a new constitution. To all intents and purposes the moment marks the birth of Spain as a uniform state, with Madrid as the center of supreme authority. During this century a red and gold national flag was adopted, a royal march chosen which became the national anthem, and a regular Spanish army formed.

There was of course an element of punishment and revenge in the obliteration of the ancient kingdom of Aragon, for Navarre and the Basque country, which had remained loyal to Philip, were allowed to retain their privileges, becoming known as the Exempt Provinces. Yet the imposition of uniformity upon Aragon and Catalonia was not entirely a one-sided affair, and throughout the century that followed, they gained as much as they lost by the arrangement. Men from these regions were granted the same opportunities as Castilians—there had been a marked inequality in many areas of life in the days of the Spanish Hapsburgs—and eventually Andalusia's monopoly of Spain's American trade was abolished in favor of a fairer distribution of trade among the ports of various regions. The Bourbon monarchs had no particular regional axe to grind: they believed in the eighteenth-century ideal of government—enlightened despotism—and centralization and conformity were essential to their aim.

Territorially Spain had suffered badly from the conditions of the Treaty of Utrecht which had ended the war. She lost her possessions in Milan, Sardinia, Naples, and the Netherlands to the Holy Roman Empire (Austria) and had been compelled to hand over Sicily to Savoy. To England she ceded Minorca and Gibraltar, the latter remaining British to the present day. Other conditions included the cession, also to Britain, of Spain's monopoly of the slave trade and the renunciation of all claims through Philip to the French throne. It was a moment of severe humiliation, but at the same time a moment of liberation. The beloved shackles had been forcibly removed and Spain was now free to concentrate upon herself and her American possessions. And this—though admittedly after a slow start—she did. Under the guidance of small groups of intelligent and farseeing men—mainly from the peripheral regions of Spain and from abroad—concerted efforts were made to bring the nation up to date, to expose her to the new winds that were blowing away the cobwebs of the past in Europe. Unfortunately, Spain's problems had roots so deep that mere good will was not enough. Supremely efficient and totally resolute direction from above was vital and it was not forthcoming. Given the circumstances, Spain's enlightened despots were not despotic enough.

In personal terms, the new regime began far from auspiciously. Philip V was an indolent melancholic who relapsed more and more frequently as the years went by into periods of lunacy. His habits became increasingly bizarre. He spent days in bed staring into space and refused to shave or change his stinking clothes for months at a time. At intervals the Escorial became the unlikely scene of wild, roistering, childish games, with the king and his dwarfs chasing after and wrestling with the queen and her ladies in waiting. Wigs rolled, bodices were ripped, faces were scratched, and hair was pulled out in handfuls. Occasionally the king indulged his eccentric pleasures even to the point of allowing his dwarfs to hurl dishes and food at their master. His partner in this extraordinary, mad twilight existence was his coarse, scheming, shrewish second wife, Elizabeth Farnese, duchess of Parma, by whom he was dominated both sexually and psychologically. Remorselessly driven by ambition, Elizabeth was prepared to submit to

any eccentricity, to any indignity, to any demands, in order to impose her own will when and where it really mattered. And Spain's active foreign policy in these years was almost entirely the fruit of her energy and sustaining will.

But an active foreign policy was the last thing Spain needed. And the country's slow start along the road to recovery after the war was directly due to Elizabeth and the equally ambitious, intriguing, almost demonic, Italian cardinal who became her chief adviser. Giulio Alberoni had wormed his way into power at the Spanish court to become the first of a series of foreigners to hold Spain's destiny in their hands in the eighteenth century. None of the others, fortunately, was to prove so devious, unscrupulous, or self-interested. Neither Alberoni nor his queen could resist the temptation of involving Spain once more in the struggle for European possessions. And their aim was not the greater glory of Spain. Elizabeth's goal was a personal one: she desperately wanted several slices of territorial cake for her two sons by Philip, neither of whom seemed likely to inherit the throne since there were half brothers nearer in line. The route she followed in pursuit of

Intermarriage was sanctioned between the Spanish colonists and the royal-blooded Indians of the New World. Here two grandees take Inca wives.

her aims was a complex one. Indeed, in Samuel Johnson's opinion, eighteenth-century international politics in Europe was too complicated for any man to understand, so suffice it to say that Elizabeth succeeded in winning back Sicily and Naples for her elder son Don Carlos. He would later exceed even her ambitions for him.

With the death of Philip, the Bourbons' scramble for personal possessions abroad came to an end and Spain herself began to receive some attention from her new monarch and his advisers. Military adventures were over for the time being, and peaceful solutions began to be seriously sought for Spain's many ills. Philip's son and heir, Ferdinand VI (*r.* 1746–1759) was himself scarcely more favored with energy and intelligence than his father—though his excesses by no means reached such colorful extremes—but both he and the nation were fortunate to possess highly capable and responsible chief ministers. In his last years, when his father's genes came to the fore and he too lost his reason, the part played by these men became significant.

For Spain the eighteenth century as a whole, however, was the era of able lieutenants. Zenón de Somodevilla, marquis of Ensenada, the first member of the Spanish aristocracy to become a Bourbon minister, who made the Spanish navy an effective force; the Irishman Bernardo Ward, who before becoming minister of commerce under Ferdinand VI toured Europe to observe foreign economic achievements and learn how best to apply them to domestic conditions; Pedro Pérez y Rodríguez, count of Campomanes, a leading economist particularly concerned with agricultural labor; Gaspar Melchor de Jovellanos, jurist, encyclopedist, poet, dramatist, and active reformer with enlightened views on all Spain's ills; the Italian Leopoldo di Gregoria, marquis of Squillaci, known to Spaniards as Esquilache, secretary of state for war and finances, whose every policy was dogged by the prejudice inspired by his foreign origin; Pedro Pablo Abarca y Bolea, count of Aranda, convinced encyclopedist, freemason, dedicated reformer, who did everything in his power to keep the Enlightenment alive in Spain; and José Moñino, count of Floridablanca, whose reforming interests embraced spheres as varied as education, industry, religion, and the navy. Such were the reactionary men who, in spite of political differences, fought to free Spain from her chauvinistic past and make her a modern European country.

In the second half of the eighteenth century, after sixty years of rule by kings unfit for the formidable task of ridding Spain of what was rotten in her society and economy, these reformers were fortunate enough to receive at last the active support of an able monarch. On his death in 1759, Ferdinand was succeeded by his half brother, Don Carlos, son of Elizabeth Farnese, who as Charles III (*r.* 1759–1788) was to earn from history the accolade of "the paradigm of enlightened despotism" in Spain. Under Charles it looked for some time as if the reforms were going to succeed.

Slowly the moribund country came once more to life. Trade and industry were encouraged and the coastal regions experienced something very closely resembling a minor industrial revolution. By the seventeenth century these areas had become more populous than the interior—a reversal of the medieval relationship—and now they also replaced Castile as Spain's source of vitality and prosperity. The privileges of the Mesta were abolished and a start was made on the enormous problems of communication created by Spain's geography, with plans for a series of canals and a network of highways. The population increased. New ideas and new philosophies began to penetrate Spain's dense traditionalism. Inspired and guided by the French *philosophes,* Spanish intellectuals read and profited from the works of Montesquieu, Hobbes, Locke, Hume, Adam Smith, and Voltaire. They eagerly embraced the latest developments in political philosophy and "discovered" political economy. This they greeted with almost religious fervor: "Behold the true philosopher's stone with which all nations can become happy," declared the new professor of political economy at the University of Saragossa. The study of science, held back in Spain by enforced fidelity to the methods of medieval scholasticism, received an enormous boost with the recognition at last that controlled experiment and observation can be science's only valid basis. Medicine improved, three observatories were built during the reigns of Ferdinand and Charles, a botanical garden was opened in Madrid in 1755, and a national museum of natural history was created. Public lectures in chemistry, physics, and mineralogy were given in Madrid, and academies of language, history, letters, science, and law were founded in the capital and elsewhere. Charles' government even sent youths to Paris to study science, engineering, and commerce.

The European Enlightenment found its way into Spain through three main channels. First, several newspapers were founded by individuals eager for reform. A notable example was the naturalist José Clavijo y Fajardo, who published *El Pensador* in imitation of Addison's *Spectator*. Secondly, the universities were compelled in the reign of Charles III to modernize their curricula and textbooks and in particular to inaugurate and encourage the study of moral philosophy, mathematics, and experimental physics. In 1774 The Council of Castile even held a contest for the best philosophy text by a Spaniard to include the theories of Descartes, Malebranche, and Leibnitz. Lastly, groups called Economic Societies of the Friends of the Country were created—again originally by an enlightened and concerned individual, Javier María Munive e Idiáquez, the count of Peñaflorida—on the model of the French *académies*; their specific aim was the encouragement of industry and agriculture, commerce, the arts and the sciences. They received the enthusiastic support of the Crown and many enjoyed considerable success in their aims. Their interests and activities were far-ranging. The Basque Society, the first official organization to be established, became actively involved in school instruction, built up a library of Spanish and foreign books, supported a knife factory, and offered a prize of one thousand *reales* for an essay on blacksmiths' bellows. Saragossa's society founded university chairs of law, moral philosophy, and civil economy and commerce, while the society at Valladolid experimented with the raising of saffron. In 1786 the Madrid Society even opened its doors to women.

One or two Spaniards enjoyed really close relationships with the philosophes, and fortunately for Spain they were in a position to make their influence felt. The count of Aranda, who became president of the Council of Castile, met Voltaire, Diderot, and D'Alembert in Paris in the 1750s, and was later able to renew the acquaintanceships as ambassador to the court of Versailles. Aranda and Voltaire exchanged gifts and eulogies. Meanwhile, the duke of Alba, who was royal ambassador to France between 1746 and 1749, was a great admirer of Jean Jacques Rousseau and in 1773 wrote to ask him to send a copy of his complete works regardless of cost. As director for twenty years of the Real Academia Española, which had been founded in 1714, Alba was important in making at least part of the new learning appear respectable.

The Crown, enlightened aristocrats, dedicated intellectuals—the Enlightenment had much working in its favor in Spain. Unhappily, however, there was more working against it. Agriculture was still the mainstay of the Spanish economy and it was choking in the deadly grip of agrarian traditions that little short of revolution could destroy. The most fertile areas of Spain's soil still languished, underexploited, in the possession of Spain's great landed gentry. What exploitation there was depended on seasonal labor only. In summer men who worked the southern *cortijos* (estates with ranch houses for the hired laborers), picking olives, sowing and reaping wheat, joined in winter the ranks of the starving unemployed. A royal official described them as follows: "They are the most unfortunate men I know in Europe. They work in the *cortijos* and olive groves when the overseers summon them. . . . Then, although nearly naked and with only the ground for a bed, they at least live on the bread and soup they are given; but when bad weather stops work . . . starving, homeless, and hopeless, they are forced to beg. . . . Half the year these men are laborers and the other half beggars."

Even in the central regions where tenant farmers were more common, short-term leases and suffocating entails ground the struggling poor down. In Castile extensive tracts of land lay uncultivated, while 150,000 beggars plagued the countryside. Spain's two largest land-owning groups—the aristocracy and the Church—lay sprawled across the body of her agriculture like some great leech, sucking it dry of all vitality. In spite of the growth of the middle class that came with the minor boom in commerce and trade, the gap between rich and poor was still enormous. And in an age when elsewhere in Europe wealth was challenging rank as the main arbiter of social position, the Spaniard clung to his dream of nobility. Minor gentry still preferred beggary to work, and Charles III's proclamation that trade and manual labor were not incompatible with honor and blue blood ("I order that nothing stand in the way of *hidalgos* supporting their families by engaging in a craft, in order to avoid the disadvantage of their living idle or badly occupied and becoming a charge on society.") made no impression on their hide-bound values. In 1787 Spain boasted one nobleman to every twenty Spaniards and most of these (480,589 to be exact) were from the minor nobility, the *hidalguía.*

Charles III, the "enlightened despot," by royal portraitist Goya

For all its rigidity, Spain's economic and social pattern would have proved more susceptible to reform and enlightenment had these not met with opposition from the country's major vested interests. Men like Aranda, Alba, and Peñaflorida were not representative of their class, most members of the aristocracy being content to lead idle, parasitic lives in ignorance of political, economic, and philosophical developments. While the nobility countered enlightenment with apathy, however, a second, perhaps more powerful, interest fought innovation with every weapon at its command. This was the Church.

In the eighteenth century the Church found itself with its back to the wall. The philosophes propagated a new approach to life and the physical world—an approach that was rational and secular. Learning was finally being cut free of its medieval scholastic moorings, experiment was replacing revelation as the criterion of knowledge, and much that the Church fathers taught was giving way before objective observation. The Christians' personal God was challenged by a deity interpreted as the sum total of the universe: and Rousseau, rejecting original sin, proclaimed the purity and nobility of man in his native state. The Enlightenment, in other words, was an unequivocal challenge to the authority of the Church, and no church as powerful as the Spanish Church could afford to ignore this threat to its political power, its material wealth, and its spiritual influence.

The issue, however, was by no means clear-cut. The history of the Spanish Church in the eighteenth century is one of conflict and high drama. The Inquisition operated independently from the Church proper much of the time, and there was a very marked division of opinion amongst the various orders as to the role that should properly be played in Church affairs by the Crown.

The Inquisition was instrumental in ensuring that what entered Spain was in fact a very watered-down version of the Enlightenment and that the number of effectively "enlightened" people remained a small minority. On the Inquisition's Index of proscribed works appeared almost all the works of the French philosophes, among them the iconoclastic bible of the Enlightenment, the *Encyclopédie* itself, edited by Diderot and D'Alembert. Few copies of the prohibited books penetrated the barrier, and they were, for the most part, accessible only to those who could read French. The ordinary Spaniard would therefore have found it difficult to come by any close acquaintance with the new ideas, even had he any inclination to do so. The agrarian and educational reformer Pablo Olavide was condemned by the Inquisition in the most famous inquisitorial trial of the century for corresponding with Voltaire and Rousseau and for holding views which in the words of the Inquisitors made him a formal heretic. Aranda, Campomanes, and Floridablanca, on the other hand, whose names were divulged by a terrified informant in a subsequent trial as followers and admirers of the French philosophes, were left to continue reading their intellectual heroes in peace. Toward the end of the century the circulation of forbidden literature did increase somewhat, though not through diminished inquisitorial scrutiny. On the contrary, it was the inevitable result of the presence on Spanish soil by the 1790s of the astonishing number of around 27,000 resident foreign families, drawn to the Peninsula throughout the century by the opportunity offered by native depopulation. Eager for news of what was happening in the world outside they found ways of smuggling in foreign books and disseminating them amongst their fellow expatriots.

For all its effectiveness in limiting the Enlightenment's impact in Spain, the Inquisition itself did not entirely escape the new liberalizing influence. The Crown resolutely enforced its traditional authority over the Holy Office in the reign of Charles III, ordering it to concern itself only with crimes of heresy and apostasy and forbidding the imprisonment of suspected persons until their guilt was proven. Inquisitors were appointed who were rather less saturated with the ultramontane attitudes of Spain's religious past, and as a result, torture and public burning of heretics became rare occurrences. The Inquisition's last victim—an old crone accused of sorcery—was burned in Seville in 1780. But abolition of the Inquisition was as yet politically impossible. For all the dread it inspired, it had become an integral part of Spain's religious life, and any threat to its existence seemed a threat to Spain's Christian civilization. So that although Aranda, as president of the Council of Castile, is said by some to have plotted to abolish the Holy Office—a plot unwittingly ruined by Voltaire, no less, who let the secret out—the government in any event left well alone after it had blunted the Inquisition's fangs. As Charles III put it, "The Spaniards want it and it does not bother me." Incredibly, the prisoner had come to love his chains, or, at least, to feel he could not live comfortably without them.

The great religious controversy in eighteenth-century Spain revolved around the difficult relationship between Church and Crown. Throughout the centuries the Crown had acquired a substantial say in ecclesiastical matters in Spain. In the reign of Charles the Bewitched, however, with a weak and ailing hand in only partial control of State affairs, the Church, particularly its Jesuit element, had managed to wrest most of its affairs from the royal grip. This situation in no way suited the new Bourbon dynasty. The concept of autocratic rule in which they believed demanded the supremacy of the Crown over the Church in secular matters. In the struggle between papal and regal authority that followed, the cause of Rome was championed by the Jesuits, who had carved out for themselves in Spain a position of power they had no intention of giving up easily; that of the Crown was supported by large numbers of ecclesiastics from other orders, motivated as much by hatred of the Jesuits as by any high principle. All these royalists were labeled indiscriminately by the Jesuits as Jansenists. In fact, while "Jansenist" had specific dogmatic connotations in France, in Spain the Jesuits used it as a dirty word to describe anybody hostile to them and their views.

The Jesuits inevitably earned the hostility of the Crown by their support of the pope. With their wealth and influence they incited the envy and antagonism of other orders, not least because of their control of the Inquisition. The country's enlightened reformers, for their part, were confirmed opponents. The Jesuits dominated the universities, holding up educational progress and deliberately using higher education to create useful connections with the aristocracy. The *Colegios mayores,* or university residences founded to house poor students, they had converted into exclusive colleges for the sons of the rich. Above all, the Jesuits were seen as representing and fomenting the religious superstitions and irrational attitudes to life that the reformers dedicated themselves to erasing from the face of Spanish society.

The Spaniards' own entrenched prejudices were a major obstacle to reform and progress, and this broad streak of deep-rooted traditionalism became intimately involved in the uproar that split the Church, the Jesuits exploiting it while enlightened ecclesiastics deprecated it.

For the most part the people stood for the *status quo*. And in Spain in
the second half of the century the *status quo* included 200,000 ecclesiastics in a population of only 10,000,000, and a fabulously rich Church
that, in the eyes of the government, mismanaged its resources disgrace-
fully. Instead of making available its vast lands for the poor to cultivate and earn a living from, the Church encouraged idleness and
beggary by dispensing alms and charity—the bishop of Granada gave
bread every day to no fewer than two thousand men and to three or
four thousand women. And the splendid church buildings were a
painful contrast with the squalid hovels and barren land that were
the lot of the innumerable poor, as a German traveler in Old Castile
in the 1790s noticed: "Uniform plains, few houses, stony and almost
barren fields, with a few vineyards here and there, numerous flocks of
sheep, few horned cattle, no meadows, no forests, no gardens nor
country houses, and in general a dreary and monotonous scene. Even
the few villages we meet with but show the misery of the inhabitants.
The houses are of mud and half ruined, the roofs, which let in the
light, loaded with stones in order to resist the wind, but the churches,
chapels, and monasteries [are] massive and magnificent."

Charles III's anticlerical ministers allowed no scales to blind their
eyes to Spain's state. Gaspar Melchor de Jovellanos despaired: "What
is left of that former glory except the skeleton of its cities, once populous and full of factories and workshops, of stores and shops, and now
only peopled by churches, convents, and hospitals, which survive
amidst the poverty they have caused?" But the mass of the common
people lived in the past and shunned anything that smacked of novelty.
To this day Spaniards answer *"No hay novedad"* when asked "How are
things?" Literally the phrase means "There's nothing new," but the
implication behind it is, "Everything's fine." Change, in other words,
is undesirable, even dangerous.

Early on under the new Bourbon dynasty, the professor of philosophy at Oviedo, a Benedictine monk called Benito Jeronimo Feijóo y
Montenegro (1676–1764), set himself the task of dispelling virtually
singlehanded the shroud of superstition and apathy which had descended upon Spanish society during the seventeenth century and
which the Jesuits were accused of encouraging for their own ends.
Even as a boy he had been skeptical of irrational, unquestioned preju-

A typical Spanish country kitchen, by Velásquez

dice and superstitions. He recalled, "When I was a boy, everyone said
that it was very dangerous to eat anything immediately after the hot
chocolate [at breakfast time]. My mind, for some reason which I could
not then perhaps have explained very well, was so skeptical of this
common apprehension that I decided to make the experiment. . . . Immediately after my chocolate, I ate a large quantity of fried salt pork,
and I felt fine that day and for a long time thereafter, wherefore I had
the satisfaction of laughing at those who were possessed by this fear."
For years he observed, experimented, and reflected. Only at the comparatively advanced age of fifty did he start to pour out his views and
his findings in a refreshing stream of sane yet eloquently impassioned
essays.

Feijóo wrote on every possible subject under the sun; he advocated
a rational, objective, and critical approach to learning, life, and even
religion. A devout Catholic like all Spain's eighteenth-century reformers, he argued that to reject Aristotle as the sole basis of learning was
not necessarily to reject religion—something that most churchmen
were finding difficult to understand. Scientific progress was not incompatible with faith, and scientific progress was what Spain needed
most of all. Religious superstition was Feijóo's special bugbear. An
admirer of Newton, Descartes, and Bacon, he could see how the social
fabric of Spain was eaten up by ignorance and absurdity of belief. False
miracles, irrational devotion to particular saints and images, he regarded as injurious to the true spiritual welfare of society, and he was
not afraid to attack those members of the Church who aided and
abetted the deception. Such was the admiration and respect he inspired
that when his writings evoked the inevitable hostile reaction from those
with a vested interest in superstition and ignorance, the king, Ferdinand VI, gave them his royal stamp of approval and forbade the publication of any criticism. "Thanks to the immortal Feijóo, spirits no
longer trouble our houses, witches have fled our towns, the evil eye
does not plague the tender child, and an eclipse does not dismay us."
So said a contemporary in recognition of Feijóo's influence. And although superstition was not of course completely extirpated by the
crusading pen of this one man, that his criticisms were welcome to
many is shown by the enormous popularity of his two collections of
essays—the *Teatro crítico universal* in nine volumes and the *Cartas*

eruditas in five. Only the tale of Spain's beloved knight-errant, *Don Quijote,* could rival them in the number of editions printed.

There was much wrong with religion in Spain—and when it suited them the Jesuits pointed it out. In 1758 a Jesuit priest, José Francisco de Isla, published a novel called *The history of the famous preacher Fray Gerundio de Campazas,* in which he made brilliant fun both of the ignorance of many of the Spanish clergy and of the stylized, rhetorical, and ornate method of preaching that was fashionable in his day. The Jesuits by now, however, were proving perilously tiresome and meddling and their enemies were on the lookout for a way of dealing with them once and for all. The opportunity came a few years later, in 1766, with a public incident that, ironically for the Jesuit order, was in part the outcome of the ultramontane attitudes they had fostered. It was the moment when Spanish traditionalism rebelled violently against the enlightened reform being imposed upon it from above.

The number of enlightened, as has already been said, remained a small, if influential, minority. And the majority, which at first had been indifferent, became, as time went by, positively hostile. For it began to be apparent that the Enlightenment and its reforms were foreign—above all, French—in origin. Many of the nobility in embracing the new ideas embraced also French dress and French customs, and introduced Gallicisms into their speech. Early on in the century a homesick Philip V had come to loathe the gloomy Escorial and had built the summer palace of La Granja to remind him of Versailles. The act was to prove symbolic of the attempt to replace Spanish traditions and standards with those of France. Spain's religious drama of the previous century, which was still alive and close to the hearts of its people, was denounced as tasteless and extravagantly irreverent, while its secular theater, descendent in tone and spirit, though not in quality of the glorious Golden Age, was despised for not conforming to the classical literary precepts.

At the center of the popular eruption, when it came, there was indeed a foreigner—albeit an Italian: the marquis of Esquilache, secretary of state for war and finance. He had already lost the confidence of the people after the Seven Years' War (1756–1763), in which Spain had lost Florida to Britain, but the years of privation after the war, due to a succession of bad harvests and high food prices, brought his reputation to an even lower ebb. His entirely admirable attempts at bettering the lot of the people by building roads and installing street lighting in Madrid were in fact fiercely resented by the taxpayers who had to finance them. And of course the usual accusations of nest-feathering and loose living were bandied about.

The straw that broke the camel's back was a very small straw indeed. In order to reduce crime, Esquilache disinterred an ancient law forbidding men to wear the dramatic, traditional Spanish long cloak and broad-brimmed hat, on the grounds that they acted as an all too effective disguise for criminals wishing to escape identification. The alternatives imposed were the short cape and the French tricorn. This attack on their traditional mode of dress was interpreted by Spaniards, particularly by the Madrid bullies who benefited most from it, as an attack on their whole way of life. On March 23, 1766—Palm Sunday—a violent mob raged through Madrid, sacked Esquilache's mansion, stoned others, pulled down the hated street lamps—ironical symbol now of the lights of progress and reform—and surged toward the royal palace itself. The following day Charles III—considerably shaken by the incident—was forced to cancel the new law, exile Esquilache, and reduce the price of food. The count of Aranda had to be called in as Esquilache's successor to put the government and the country back on an even keel. He later achieved part of the desired reform, in Madrid at least, with a shrewd piece of legislation—the broad-brimmed hat was made the official uniform of the executioner!

The suddenness and ferocity of the incident—called the Mutiny of Esquilache—suggested to many that it had been deliberately provoked by elements hostile to Esquilache and the Enlightenment in general. Whatever the truth of the matter, a scapegoat was found— the Jesuits. A royal commission pronounced them guilty of incitement to riot and in the following year the Jesuit order was expelled from Spain. The Church for the most part approved, the people raised not a murmur, and all discussion of the affair was prohibited by royal order. Within ten years, the last of Charles' foreign advisers was dispatched, a small sop to public opinion now that the Crown had rid itself of the main opponent to regalistic policy. And in 1773 France and Spain managed to "persuade" the pope to suppress the Jesuit order completely.

This uprise of nationalist feeling is of peculiar interest because it marks the birth of what has become to tourists all over the world the "typical" Spain, the Spain of the tourist poster. The lower classes were not in a position to see the advantages of influences from abroad. All they saw was the betrayal of their heritage, of Spanish life, symbolized in the dress, speech, and manners of those who aped the French, and they came to loathe and despise the fashionable gentleman (or *peti-metre* as they called him from *petit maître*) with his wig, tricorn hat, and waisted coat—for them a mincing, emasculated figure. In reaction they deliberately cultivated those aspects of Spanish life which were most opposed to the world of the French *salon* and most representative of their own Spanishness. The bullfight—frowned upon by the Crown and by enlightened intellectuals—received a new lease of popularity, and in becoming a popular, rather than an aristocratic, pastime, evolved gradually into the sort of stylized and theatrical entertainment it is today. The amateur *matador* displaying his skill and courage in front of his noble peers and the ladies of the court was replaced by the pro-

fessional matador from the lower classes. By the end of the century the bullfight had arrived at the form with which we are familiar today—except that dogs were used to goad lazy, bored, or just cowardly bulls into action—and had begun to produce folk heroes and *aficionados*. One of the earliest matadors lionized by the people was Pepe Hilo (José Delgado), "whose chest seemed to measure three feet from shoulder to shoulder." He was a great favorite with the women, and when he was killed in the bull ring in Madrid on May 11, 1801, all Spain mourned.

Religious festivals, such as the Holy Week processions, were celebrated with renewed fervor as the spectators and participants sought in them a confirmation of their Spanish identity. And the fashionable lower classes of Madrid, called *majos* and *majas,* made a cult of wearing what seemed to them the national costume. Certainly it distinguished them from the hated "Frenchies," and several elements of it came to symbolize the so-called Spanish national dress. The *majo* strutted around in breeches, a short jacket, a sash that concealed a fold-

The haughty pride of the Spanish aristocrat is evident in these Goya portraits.

ing knife, a broad-brimmed or high and pointed round hat, and a long cape. He wore his long hair in a net and smoked a huge, black cigar —taboo in elegant society as being a filthy, antisocial habit. The *maja* favored a full-skirted, low-necked costume with a small shawl round the shoulders and crossed over the bosom and, on special occasions, a high comb and lace mantilla. She, too, often carried a weapon—a small poniard tucked into her left garter. Fortunately for us Goya has recorded for posterity the arrogant elegance of these swaggering dandies who, for all their humble origins, regarded themselves as purer Spaniards than the upper classes, and therefore intrinsically superior to them. Ostentatiously epitomizing the attitudes that were wholly Spanish, and proud of the fact, they became the heroes and heroines of the lower classes, a symbol of national pride at a time when the government was trying to convince them that Spain was rotten and backward and that "abroad" and its ways were the source of all well-being.

This was a message, as we have seen, that those concerned for Spain's welfare were prepared to believe, and it was a message that gradually, for all the opposition, for all the watering down of the processes of enlightenment, began to have its salutary effects. And the medicine of reform would undoubtedly have continued to work upon the various national malaises but for the event that in 1789 rocked the civilized world—the French Revolution. Many of Spain's so-called progressives reacted like scalded cats. If this was what enlightenment led to, then they wanted no part of it.

By now a new king had ascended the throne. Charles III had died in 1788 and had been succeeded by his inadequate son, Charles IV (*r.* 1788–1808), whose vapid face peers down at us from Goya's ruthlessly revealing portraits of the Spanish royal family. At a time when the country desperately needed a strong guiding hand to steer it through the fears and uncertainties inspired in a Europe shocked by the French Terror, Spain had the misfortune to be dealt an inexperienced, unintelligent monarch completely in the control of his waspish, randy, fishwife of a consort, María Luisa—grand-daughter, appropriately enough, of Elizabeth Farnese. Not unnaturally the Crown, and the reforming intellectuals who supported it, regarded with gloom the assault on autocratic government that was taking place just across the border. Floridablanca wrote of France: "It is said that this enlightened country has taught man his rights. But it has also taken away, besides his true happiness, peace and the security of his person and family. We want here neither so much light nor its effects: insolent acts, words and writings against legitimate authority." Silence was imposed on the Revolution and on all news from Paris; newspapers were suppressed, strict watch was kept on the frontier to prevent any revolutionary tentacles from creeping in, and every foreigner to enter Spain was made to swear to an oath of allegiance to the throne and to Catholicism.

For Spain it was a moment of crisis and of destiny; France pressed for an open declaration of her intentions and affiliations, and the future of Spain hung in the balance. At this moment Charles IV chose to get rid of the last of his father's able ministers. Appointed in his stead was Manuel Godoy, a handsome, twenty-five-year-old ex-guards officer whom María Luisa, twice his age and mother of a large brood of royal children, had made her lover. For many aristocrats, particularly the ladies, Godoy, who was fond of society and entertaining, was a welcome and lively addition to the dreary, monotonous round of the Spanish court—that "pompous and empty machine," as a foreign observer accustomed to the social and intellectual glitter of Versailles, Vienna, Berlin, and Saint Petersburg called it. But the sniggering scorn heaped on the foolish cuckold king brought the Spanish monarchy for the first time into disrespect with the common people—even poor Charles the Bewitched had managed to command their loyalty. As the much-diminished band of enlightened thinkers desperately fought to prevent Spain's substantial achievements from being thrown away in a moment of panic, another momentous piece of news from Paris forced Spain to declare her hand. Louis XVI had been guillotined. The crowned heads of Europe trembled for their royal necks. Spain accordingly declared herself against the Republic, and war with France broke out.

The people were jubilant at the decision to fight the satanic forces of revolution. The advance of French troops into Spanish territory soon helped change their minds, and when Godoy signed a treaty with France, the country—through María Luisa—saw fit to reward his compliance with the title of Prince of the Peace. The title turned sour indeed when peace with France proved to mean war with England. From now on Spain was forced to dance to the tune that her revolutionary neighbor called—"when France sneezes, Spain is bound to answer 'Bless

OVERLEAF: *Goya's "Third of May," in which French soldiers execute Spanish freedom fighters, chronicles the bloody aftermath of the Madrid riot in 1808.*

you.' " The nation had been sold into a slavery from which only violence would liberate it.

Under Godoy's mismanagement Spain was outmaneuvered completely by the French; with Napoleon now in power, the Prince of the Peace was fighting sadly outside his league. After losing Trinidad to the English, Spain was forced to concede Louisiana to her so-called ally France. Like the pawn he had become, Godoy was removed from power, then put back again. Finally, under pressure from France, Spain invaded Portugal, which unlike Spain was still hostile to the new France.

Napoleon sent Godoy fifteen thousand troops to help him overthrow the Portuguese, and in the face of the combined Spanish and French advance, Portuguese opposition collapsed. Godoy in turn sent María Luisa the branch of an orange tree as a victor's trophy, and the military "walk over" was dubbed the War of the Oranges by way of insult. So far everything had gone well and Godoy was made commander in chief of the army and navy. The trouble came when Godoy informed Napoleon that he could now withdraw his troops from the Peninsula. The answer came back, "Is the king tired of reigning?" And if there had been any doubt as to its meaning, the arrival of further contingents of French troops soon dispelled any doubts. Spain itself had been invaded.

Although the troops were subsequently withdrawn from a suitably impressed Spain, humiliation followed humiliation. France confirmed England's possession of Trinidad without even consulting Spain; she sold Louisiana to the United States although she had guaranteed never to alienate the territory; and Godoy was forced to buy neutrality from Napoleon. Gradually hate and resentment of French arrogance began to smolder and spark in Spain. The opposition found a focus in the heir to the throne, Prince Ferdinand, who hated his mother and loathed her lover Godoy even more. When war broke out with England in 1804 and Lord Nelson made mincemeat of the Spanish fleet at the Battle of Trafalgar on the southwest coast of Spain, the disaster into which Godoy had dragged Spain was forcibly brought home to the Spanish people. Yet unbelievably, Godoy had not finished. Oblivious to the lesson he should have learned from the invasion of Portugal some years before, he signed a second pact with Napoleon aimed at bringing Por-

An allegorical portrait of Colombia and Simón Bolívar, El Libertador, who secured the nation's independence from Spain in 1819

tugal—once more proving recalcitrant—to its knees for good. In the hope that southern Portugal would be his personal reward, Godoy blindly and stupidly accepted a guarantee that Spain's independence would remain inviolate when French troops crossed into Portugal.

In fact Napoleon's armies had already crossed the Pyrenees. And as soon as Portugal had been annexed to France, the invaders proceeded to occupy the north of Spain. Godoy, to give him his due, was in favor of resistance, but Charles IV shrank from the challenge. In March, 1808, the royal family fled to the summer palace at Aranjuez, their delightful retreat in happier days; and Prince Ferdinand, who had already plotted to dethrone his craven, puppetlike father, savored a brief moment of triumph. A raging mob sacked Godoy's house as he hid, trembling for his life, in a roll of matting. Charles, reaping the harvest of his years of eunuchoid passivity, had no alternative but to abdicate, but for Spain and for Ferdinand the gesture came too late. By the time the new king had returned to his capital, as Ferdinand VII, Madrid was in the hands of the French.

Faced with this new dilemma the royals scrambled ignominiously for Napoleon's favor. Charles IV asked Napoleon to get him back his throne and Ferdinand set out to meet the emperor in order to secure his own cause. The projected meeting proved to be a trap and Ferdinand was "detained" at the emperor's pleasure in Bayonne. There at this point the whole family assembled—Ferdinand himself, Charles and María Luisa together with Godoy—to plead for the power and position that were theirs by right. Playing Ferdinand and Charles off against each other, Napoleon made sure that he alone remained the victor. Ferdinand was compelled to abdicate in favor of his father and Charles to abdicate in favor of Napoleon. Spain was experiencing the ultimate betrayal.

But Spain had no intention of meekly submitting any longer to the emperor's design. She had no wish to be governed by Napoleon's brother Joseph Bonaparte, to whom the throne had been given, and who was picturesquely dubbed Pepe Botellas, or Joe Bottles, by his irreverent new subjects. For all their scorn for Charles and Godoy, the Spanish people were enraged at the news that their royal family had been deported to France. On May 2, 1808, the Madrid populace, armed with sticks, axes, picks—anything they could lay their hands on—rose as one against the hated intruder. The glory and horror of the *Dos de Mayo,* as the occasion has gone down in Spanish history, have been recorded in all their gruesome vividness on the darkly massive canvases of Goya, and the moment is justifiably one of Spain's proudest memories. The nationalism and love of tradition that had made so much of Spain turn its face resolutely against the tide of progress were now, in the hour of need, to prove its salvation. Once Madrid had set the example, the whole of Spain would not rest until the foreigners had been banished from Spanish soil. The cost was high, for Spain became the battleground for Europe's stand against Napoleon's tyranny when Great Britain answered Spain's appeal for help and dispatched the duke of Wellington to launch what has become known to the world as the Peninsular War, though for the Spaniards it has always been their War of Independence. Spain's faith in its own monarchy would turn out to be a bitter disillusion, but at least the country would feel able to hold its head up again beneath the world's gaze. It might mismanage its own affairs, but it would not be a mere pawn in those of others. As for Napoleon, Spain was his undoing. In Spain, and with the help of Spain, particularly Spanish guerilla fighters, England and Wellington gave the great man the first serious hint of the nemesis which he soon met at Waterloo. Later on in his prison on Saint Helena, Napoleon would look back and realize that in pushing the Spanish people one step too far along the road to abject humiliation he had prepared his own downfall. Spain the giant-killer was revenged indeed for the centuries of French rivalry, interference, and domination. Only the wisdom of hindsight shows how bittersweet the revenge was. For Napoleon's predatory invasion of Spain had driven Spaniards to seek a solution to their problems in violence: it was a solution to which they would turn repeatedly in the years to come.

CHAPTER VII

THE EMERGENCE
OF THE
TWO SPAINS

T he history of Spain between the French-influenced eighteenth century and that terrible explosion in 1936—the Spanish civil war—is the history of a country trying to find itself. It is a confused and confusing period. It is the period when one Spain struggled painfully to give birth to the liberalism whose seed had been implanted by the Enlightenment; and another, darker, Spain desperately fought to ensure that the bright new child of the future died in infancy, smothered by the weight of tradition, intolerance, and reaction. Napoleon's attack had not only brought the Bourbon dynasty to its knees, it had also wrenched Spain away from the continuity of the past and placed her on the threshold of a different world, a new future. The way was open for a fresh start and there were many prepared to take it. But to break with the past is not to destroy it, and in Spain opinions differed violently on how to build up a new Spain on the ruins of the old.

The opportunity to make of the future something very different from the past was created by that very surge of nationalist feeling that first of all kept revolution out of Spain and subsequently drove the Corsican tyrant back over the Pyrenees. The ignominious departure of the

Saragossa is remembered as one of the last brave towns to hold out against Napoleon's troops.

royal family and the Peninsular War that followed in effect opened the door to the ideas from which Spain was seeking to preserve herself. The Spanish people, to their disgust left to the mercy of a foreign commoner, Joseph Bonaparte, decided to manage without a monarch and govern their own affairs. As the opposition to the French exploded into revolt, regional *juntas* or committees were set up all over Spain to organize the resistance, train militias, and run the provinces their own way. For the first time since the Middle Ages the Spanish people were taking their fate into their own hands and claiming a say in the running of their lives. And as if to prove that history indeed repeats itself, the first region to take such action was Asturias, cradle of Spanish resistance to another invader more than a thousand years before.

The step the Spanish people took was a brave and fateful one, brave because of its boldness and newness, fateful because of its consequences: for by introducing liberalism into Spain, a country with a strong religious and monarchic tradition, they were setting light to a veritable keg of gunpowder. For the rest of the century, Spain would be free of foreign interference, yet at the same time more riven by internal strife and civil war than any other nation in Europe. A vacant throne and a totally disrupted social order allowed liberals and reformers in these early years to rethink Spain's political structure from scratch, unhampered as yet by the shadow of revolution or treason. The result, after a meeting of the Cortes in Cádiz in 1812, was a constitution for a new Spain, in which the Cortes itself would be the seat of legislative power and the only depository of sovereignty.

The new charter, in support of which many men were to sacrifice their lives in the years to come, was only mildly revolutionary. It proposed a united Spain, with a common law and common taxation for all, governed by a constitutional monarchy and an elected Cortes which would meet for three months every year; nothing, one might justifiably think, which would provoke heated opposition or present much difficulty in effectuating. The trouble was, political affiliation in Spain came in as many shades as the Biblical Joseph's many-colored coat. Even the Spain that rose up against the French was a nation sorely divided. There were those—admittedly a minority—for whom Napoleon was the best thing that had happened to Spain in a long while and who welcomed his brother Joseph Bonaparte with open arms. These

Afrancesados were far outnumbered, of course, by those who remained loyal to the exiled Spanish royal family. In addition to the royalists of either side, there were liberals of varying degrees of liberality—conservative liberals, liberal liberals, and revolutionary liberals. There were even Godoyists—people who looked forward to the day when María Luisa's Prince of the Peace would be back in power.

The reformers who met at Cádiz to draft the new constitution were themselves divided into a left wing, the "liberals," and a right wing, the "serviles." The revolutionary vision of the left was soon watered down into the modest declaration of rights already described, called the Constitution of Cádiz. As was so often to happen in the years to come, the dedicated reformers wanted their new Spain there and then, and they tilted with imprudent haste at attitudes and institutions too deeply rooted in Spanish society to be summarily plucked out one fine day without fierce resentment.

At the center of the problem was that perpetual Spanish bogey, religion—or rather, in this instance, clericalism. The clash came early on. At the discussions at Cádiz a move was made by the liberals to abolish the Inquisition—a feature of Spanish life which even Charles III, as we saw, had not dared remove. The Spanish bishops were adamant in opposing the measure and a majority of delegates supported them. From this point on, liberalism came to be equated in the minds of Spaniards with the idea of an entirely secular state and later, by extension, with such horrors as Darwinism, Protestantism, Freemasonry, and Agnosticism, even Atheism. Some impression of the fear and revulsion inspired in the Spanish clergy and hence in a very large number of ordinary Spaniards in the nineteenth century by the word "liberal" can be got from the following threat, published in a Madrid newspaper in 1871 several years after the appearance of a Vatican encyclical denouncing liberal views: "As the Virgin Mother of the Saviour of men crushed with her pure feet the head of the infernal Serpent, so Pius IX will also crush with his Syllabus the head of Liberalism, the true Serpent of the nineteenth century." To make sure that those with liberal leanings were in no doubt as to the seriousness of their crime, the Catechism duly reminded them from the age of childhood upward: "What sin is committed by him who votes for a liberal candidate?" "Generally a mortal sin."

In 1814 the exiled Ferdinand VII, whose coming had been so long awaited by so many Spaniards, moderate liberals included, returned to occupy the throne won back for him after six years of occupation and war by his faithful subjects. He was the prince in shining armor who would usher in a period of hope and peaceful progress, the kingpin of the new constitution; a figure, it seemed, who would contrive to satisfy left and right, traditionalist and reformer. He turned out to be the most contemptible king Spain had the misfortune to inherit: a congenital reactionary without an unselfish impulse in his body and no conception of the meaning of progress and reform. Two days before he entered Madrid, a royal decree was promulgated annulling the constitution, and all those known to have played an active part in its formation were arrested. By all standards of honesty and integrity it was an illegal act, but the constitution had not provided for the contingency of royal disobedience. It had in fact declared: "The king's person is sacred and inviolable, and is not subject to responsibility"; and the men whose brainchild it was were now paying the bitter price of their loyalty and optimism. Surrounding himself with the mediocre and the sycophantic, the new king proceeded to govern like the unenlightened despot he was. He did not lack support. Many—traditionalists, clericalists, and army men—could hardly wait for him to set foot in Spain before urging him to the repressive steps he was only too inclined to take. As for the majority of Spanish people, ingrained monarchists still and deliriously happy to have their own king back, they were unable to look beyond the security of the traditional order to their own best interests. "Death to liberty and the constitution," they shouted in the streets as they welcomed back their beloved jailor. And their wish was granted.

For six years Spain experienced once again the degradation, the benighted mismanagement, the abuse of restored rights and privileges of the worst years of the seventeenth century. The country became the sacrificial lamb on the altar of political chicanery and self-interest; life within it resembled the sort of existence we now associate with the modern police state. The liberals who had fought for Spain while their exiled king actually congratulated Napoleon on his victories, were now driven to seek refuge in the very country they had fought. Twelve thousand people were sentenced to perpetual exile in a single decree, amongst them many of the foreign families who had made homes in

Joseph Bonaparte, would-be constitutional monarch, managed to keep his dignity and the Spanish throne for a mere five years before France's rout in 1813.

Spain. Rigid censorship of books and newspapers was imposed, spies everywhere inhibited and poisoned the natural flow of everyday life, and the very existence of the Cortes was conveniently forgotten.

The effect of this suffocating regime was momentous, so momentous that Spain is still suffering from it today. Although Spain since the Middle Ages had had no tradition of popular representation or political institutionalism on which to build, the liberal leaders were eager to bring about almost at a stroke the brave new world they envisaged for their country. The oppression to which Ferdinand subjected Spain drove them to despair of any peaceful solution to the tension between reaction and reform. So they resorted to violence, and in doing so they enrolled the help of the liberal elements in the Spanish army. This step was taken in 1820 and was to have an impact they could not possibly have anticipated at the time. Without realizing it, they had loosed upon the Spanish political scene a lion that would never again submit to captivity. Once the army knew the sweet taste of political power it would refuse to relinquish it; and although they entered the struggle on the liberal side, "nowadays," as a Spanish commentator pointedly remarked, "the soldiers are on the other side of the barricade." The precedent thus established gave rise to the emergence of the Spanish army as one of the country's foremost political parties. For that was what, in effect, it rapidly became.

At first, however, the army, under the liberal military leader, Rafael del Riego, brought back the constitution by force. His *pronunciamiento* (Spain's word for a military *coup d'état*), the first of many in the nineteenth and twentieth centuries, was staged on January 1, 1820. (Riego's military march, the *Himno de Riego* composed in his honor, became the musical inspiration of Spanish liberalism throughout the country. Later on, under the Second Republic in the 1930s, it would become the official national anthem.) For a while King Ferdinand was forced to behave himself. "Let us advance frankly, myself leading the way, along the constitutional path," he enjoined his subjects, not believing or meaning a word of what he said. His lack of cooperation and attempts to stir up trouble, together with the hostility of many of his subjects toward the new regime, dogged the efforts of those who were trying to govern constitutionally. Gradually the country started to slide into anarchy and civil strife as disagreement, disorder, and disillusion choked the liberal ideals to which the enthusiastic had thought to woo the Spanish people overnight. They had forgotten that to build without foundations is a task requiring painstaking care and ingenuity.

Meanwhile, in France revolution and progressive dictatorship had given way once again to monarchy, and keen interest was taken in the unexpected turn of events in the Peninsula. Spain had now become the source of contagion that other European monarchies wished to insulate themselves from; the *cordon sanitaire* thrown across the Spanish border by Louis XVIII in 1822 was to protect the north from Spanish liberalism as much as from the dreaded yellow fever rampaging through the Peninsula. France, being the most conveniently placed as well as the most vulnerable nation involved, was chosen by the other interested countries, Austria, Russia, and Prussia, for the job of restoring order in Spain. And so in 1823 the Spaniards saw French troops once again march through their country—"the hundred thousand sons of Saint Louis," as they derisively dubbed them. This time, though, there was no resistance, no revolt; the foreigners were now coming to the rescue of tradition.

Ferdinand lost no time in making up for his years of "most ignominious slavery." Riego—liberalism's first martyr—was hanged, drawn, and quartered, hundreds of his supporters went to the gallows, and 35,000 French troops remained at Spain's own expense to maintain the king's law and order. The tyranny of oppression and perverted mediocrity descended upon Spain once more. A spokesman of the University of Cervera considered it prudent to begin a loyal address with the words "Far from us the dangerous novelty of thinking."

The ding-dong struggle between left and right, between the Establishment and the reformers, becomes from now on the characteristic feature of nineteenth-century Spain. Against a backdrop of appalling royal inadequacy, agrarian troubles, emerging socialism, and imperial decay, the military politicians of both liberal and conservative persuasions, the generals Baldomero Espartero, Ramón Narváez, Leopoldo O'Donnell, Francisco Serrano, and Juan Prim, to name only the best known, fought their battle for the future of Spain. It is a story far too labyrinthine to follow step by step and too disheartening in its repetitiveness. The whole issue was complicated by the fact that the monarchists were themselves divided. For many, Ferdinand was not absolute enough. Furthermore, the Church disapproved of the fact that he made no move to re-establish the Inquisition, suppressed under the constitution between 1820 and 1823; while the regions of the north and east—the Basque country, Navarre, Aragon, and Catalonia—where regionalism had always been strong, saw no chance of his supporting the resuscitation of their privileges. The "apostolics," as these discontented reactionaries were called, accordingly looked for another leader. They found him in Ferdinand's younger brother Don Carlos.

The challenge to King Ferdinand might not have come to anything but for an accident of fate, dreaded by hereditary monarchs, which left its imprint deep on the face of nineteenth-century Spain—Ferdinand had no sons. Traditionally, Spanish law permitted women to inherit the throne, but the Bourbons had brought with them the French Salic law permitting only male descendants to ascend the throne, though this had been secretly rescinded in 1789 by Charles IV. With the succession in doubt and popular support for Don Carlos growing daily, the last years of King Ferdinand—who was in his own words "the cork in the beer bottle"—were fraught with intrigue at court. The moderates and surviving liberals flocked to the support of Ferdinand's baby daughter Isabella; and out of the rage inspired in his opponents by this new hindrance to their plans, the Carlist movement was born.

Isabella's coronation on her father's death in 1833 solved nothing. A civil war broke out which lasted for seven years, and which in its turn settled nothing. Under the banner of Carlism there assembled everyone who saw in liberalism and the constitution a betrayal of all that Spain had stood for in the days of her greatness—an absolute monarchy independent of Europe and dedicated to Catholicism. Within such a monarchy, united in loyalty and faith, the regions could live their own traditional lives faithful to the memory of those days when regions were kingdoms. Carlism in other words was nostalgia for the past, and as such exerted an attraction for Spaniards which has not yet died out. In the 1850s and the 1870s Spain was torn twice more by Carlist civil wars, and still today there is a Carlist claimant to Spain's unoccupied throne.

If Ferdinand's death created problems which were to reverberate through Spanish society for decades to come, it was also a moment of liberation and of opportunity for those with political ideals and a social consciousness, one of those clearly discernible moments in Spanish history when a door has opened in the wall of her physical and spiritual isolation to admit the smell and flavor of life outside. With the succession, hundreds of exiles returned, bringing not only renewed enthusiasm for the liberal ideal, but its sister movement, Romanticism.

Spain's love affair with European Romanticism was a rather special and curious one in that she helped feed the Romantic movement as well as partaking of it. The Romantics of England, France, and Germany, in their search for the picturesque and the exotic, discovered the sun-baked Moorish Spain of popular imagination, where, in ignorance of the Industrial Revolution, the peasant still tilled the soil with a Roman plow. Famous travelers like Washington Irving, George Borrow, and Richard Ford explored Spain, her customs, traditions, and history and, in their different but equally fascinating and eloquent ways, presented their findings to an eager world. Spain, in turn, absorbed the new developments in art, literature, and music from abroad. The relationship between Spanish liberalism and Romanticism was melodramatically symbolized by the Byronic poet, José de Espronceda, who in 1830 fought for his beliefs at the Paris barricades.

But Spain has never adopted wholesale the great cultural movements of European history: she has always adapted them to suit her own peculiar interests and needs. And Romanticism experienced a similar fate in Spain. The country produced its clutch of feverish, posturing poets—Espronceda and José Zorrilla among them—who, for all their inflated rhetoric and overcultivated sensibilities, could, at times, produce work of memorable quality. But the really significant product of Spanish Romanticism—*costumbrismo*—was something very different in that it did maintain close contacts with objective reality. *Costumbrismo* may be described as the cult of the picturesque detail of everyday Spanish life, the discovery of the "real" Spain by and for Spaniards. Its intrinsic interest is now largely limited to that of the colorful documentary instructive to the social historian, yet its place in the development of Spanish prose is an important one in that it prepared the way for the great realistic novels of the second half of the nineteenth century. Its prime exponent, Mariano José de Larra, was exceptionally talented—a young man of intense concern for Spain and great clarity of judgment, with an eloquent pen and a formidable gift for satire. Before he shot himself in a fit of despair after an unhappy love affair at the age of twenty-eight, he poured his criticisms and impressions of the Spanish scene into a series of stringent and predominantly pessimistic articles. He was the first of Spain's great "involved" journalists, and another link in the long chain of Spain's disillusioned writers. "Here lies half Spain;" he wrote in one of his lampoons, "it died of the other half." How true the tragically poignant epitaph was to prove!

Larra's suicide in 1837 prevented his ever knowing how justified his fears and premonitions for his country were. At the time, Spain's queen was only seven years old, too young to give any sure intimation of the disastrous monarch she was to become. But at the still tender age of thirteen, Queen Isabella II, a contemptible successor for her first great namesake, came of age and began to rule. Her coming of age, as a Spanish historian has remarked, was "a pure constitutional fiction. Queen Isabella was never of age, though she died a grandmother." In the early decades of her long reign, plump, comely, apparently easy-going and plain-spoken, without pretension or refinement, intelligence or education, she was a great favorite of her subjects. But as the passing years revealed more and more of the willful, intriguing, and self-indulgent reality behind the lavishly dressed and dimpled exterior, her popularity waned and the initial respect she commanded was whittled away. She became known as "that impossible lady."

Hers was yet another reign of remorseless palace intrigue. A child queen, she was inevitably the immediate prey of court plotters, and, trained in such a school, she grew up to recognize no other form of political procedure. Even at thirteen she lied her first minister out of office and into exile and brought about the collapse of the government. The minister, she claimed, had forced her to sign a decree of which she disapproved. As yet, however, her gift for intrigue was nowhere near perfected. Had it been, she would not have undermined her claim with the admission that as the minister left her presence she had given him as a gift for his daughter one of the boxes of chocolates that, throughout her life, always lay scattered about the royal palace.

The people with the first access to her ear were her confessor and the discredited Sor Patricinio. The "Bleeding Nun," as the latter became known (her hands and feet were said to bear the marks of Christ's wounds), had through temperamental strength alone survived prosecu-

The nineteenth century's romantic fascination with Spain is evident in this ethereal rendering of the interior of Burgos Cathedral.

tion for fraud to see better and more powerful days. For years the fate of Spain lay effectively in the hands of people such as these, for Isabella, willful as she was, regarded as gospel truth virtually anything that came out of the mouth of a person wearing a religious habit. As a result, government in Spain, during the thirty-eight years of her reign, became nothing more than the rule of royal whim and clerical spite. An American observer, John Hay, remarked, "A safe word whispered by a crawling confessor, an attack of nerves on a cloudy day, the appearance of a well-made soldier at a levee, have often sufficed to make and break administrations." Spain's great recorder of the political and social scene, the novelist Benito Pérez Galdós, summed up as follows the arbitrary and mysterious workings of government: "Suddenly, when no one was expecting it, the government fell. *Quare causa?* No one knew; and what was worse, no one asked. We had become accustomed to governments coming and going for no other reason than the whims and fancies of the *Señora*." And as the years went by, the situation got worse, not better. Of the period around 1870 John Hay observed: "Never in all the darkest periods of Spanish history, was the reign of superstition as absolute and tyrannical as in the alcazar of Madrid during the later years of Isabel of Bourbon."

If Isabella lost the support of ministers, civil servants, and intellectuals because of her unstable and unconstitutional procedures, her popularity with the people waned largely for another reason. Respect and admiration for the charismatic royal presence cannot, especially when that presence is female, survive sexual ridicule. John Hay's "well-made soldier" provides the clue. Unlike England's youthful and beloved Queen Victoria, who was giving her country an example of what wifely devotion and female modesty should be, Spain's Isabella soon proved to have a precocious and roving eye. For reasons of state she was married, very much against her will, to a cousin, a eunuchoid youth with a squeaky voice who was soon christened "Paquita"—most adequately translated perhaps as "Fanny." "I'll marry him if he's a man," the nubile young queen at last conceded, but although the marriage indeed took place, the condition imposed by Isabella remained unresolved. No matter, marriage was what counted; for fears had been voiced that "if we don't hurry, the heir will arrive on the scene before the husband." And heirs there were—nine of them in all, to the increasing amazement and disillusion of poor Fanny. Fanny may not have been a father, but he was no fool. Convinced that the first child was not of his doing, he threatened to denounce his wife to the nation. Only quick thinking and a lot of tact prevented the Spanish throne from becoming the laughingstock of Europe. Of the nine children only four survived in the dark, damp, airless, and none-to-sweet-smelling palace, a misfortune which ironically won back for Isabella some of the sympathy formerly felt for her—"the lady of tragic destiny," as she was with some accuracy called, was one of her kinder labels.

Spain's patience with the errant queen was not inexhaustible. Three decades of political corruption and instability—1851 alone saw the dissolution of one parliament and the suspension twice over of another—created an engulfing sense of disillusion with monarchy as well as with the constitution and the processes of democracy. The increase in economic activity caused by the advent of the steam engine in Spain —between 1848 and 1858, 500 miles or so of railway track was laid, followed by 3,000 more in the next decade—served only to confuse the issue even further. There blew up around the Queen Mother, María Cristina—accused with various others of using railway-building contracts to feather her own nest—scandals so ugly that in 1854 she fled the country to the roar of an outraged populace and press demanding her head. The antiroyal storm was gathering. In 1868 it broke. The navy and army, tired of Isabella and her succession of favorites, rose against her, producing a manifesto meaningfully called "Spain with Honor," which maintained that "the person charged with the defense of the constitution should not be its irreconcilable enemy." A guard of honor of loyal army engineers escorted her across the border into France; she left with a parting quip into which she managed to inject not a little dignity, "I thought I had struck deeper roots in this land." The "impossible lady" had gone.

If everybody had wished Isabella gone, nobody knew for certain what he wanted to replace her with. The political leaders of the moment, Generals Serrano and Prim, failed to get the various political groups to agree, and the problem was handed over to the Cortes to solve. Within the year, a new constitution was drawn up which daringly legalized civil marriage and allowed foreigners, and Spaniards who formally renounced Catholicism, the privilege of religious free-

dom. Like the earlier constitution, it advocated that Spain be ruled by a constitutional monarchy. But where to find one? For a year Spain cast around Europe for a king, while the country threatened to disintegrate into anarchy. The search eventually bore results: for Europe, the Franco-Prussian War, when France objected to a projected German candidate for the throne; for Spain, a king, Amadeo of Savoy, persuaded into the task against his better judgment. Amadeo's instinct was right. Spain was not a country to take on lightly: the provisional government in the space of a year had had to contend with republican risings in Catalonia and Cádiz and a new outbreak of Carlist guerrilla activities. Queen Victoria of England had been adamant that no son of hers should take on the formidable task. As General Grey wrote in a letter to Lord Stanley: "Different Parties in Spain may combine to overthrow the Throne of Queen Isabella; but does our experience of Span-

The bullfight, a traditional exercise of Spanish courage, as seen in the mid-nineteenth century

ish Statesmen warrant the hope, that, their object effected, they will continue to act in harmony, or agree amongst themselves as to the Government to be set up? The Spaniards, besides, are proverbially indisposed to foreigners; so that an English Prince, accepting the offer of the Crown in the present circumstances, would probably find himself supported by one part of the nation, and violently opposed by another, and would thus become the cause of fresh civil wars and calamities in that unhappy country. The queen need not say how much it would distress her to see one of her sons in such a position."

Amadeo, well-meaning, earnest, and upright, lived to experience the wisdom of these remarks. The son of Italy's King Victor Emmanuel II, he was never forgiven for not being a Spaniard, and was often referred to as "the foreigner." His short-lived reign was doomed from the start: on the very day he arrived in his new country, his main supporter, Prim, was assassinated. Extreme right and left, and republicans, conspired against him to render constitutional government out of the question. With the liberals divided and socialism daily gathering momentum, especially in Barcelona, Amadeo soon found himself in an impossible situation, a reluctant traveler foundering on the quicksand of Spanish politics. In April, 1872, Don Carlos in France waved aloft the banner of Carlism, summoning all loyal Spaniards to his cause, and plunged the country into the third Carlist civil war. Amadeo, the Gentleman King, as he was known to his subjects, was by now more than ready to admit defeat and in the same year he washed his hands of Spain and abdicated. No king has probably ever relinquished his crown with a greater sense of relief, though—a gentleman to the last—he "thanked Spain for the great honor it had bestowed on him."

At this juncture Spain decided to undergo the great experiment— early in the following year the Cortes voted to make Spain a republic. Yet again, the Cortes failed to agree on matters of form and procedure, and in its first year the First Spanish Republic had no fewer than four presidents. Declared vaguely to be a federal republic, the country was threatened by a new wave of regionalist feeling already released by the civil war. Catalonia went so far as to declare itself an independent state, and Andalusia for a while dissolved into a collection of city-states. Since this piecemeal disintegration had to be rectified with force, Spain to all intents and purposes found itself ravaged by two civil wars at once. The whole country by now was so sick of anarchy masquerading as political freedom that when Isabella's son Alfonso, a sixteen-year-old cadet at Britain's Sandhurst Royal Military Academy, offered himself to his people as a constitutional monarch, as "a good Spaniard, a good Catholic, and a liberal," even the separatist Catalans gave him a joyous welcome. Urged on by the century's last coup in the king's favor, Spain gladly turned back the clock and gave up the exhausting burden of liberty in favor of Alfonso XII (*r.* 1874–1885).

This time, the course for a truly constitutional monarchy and a democratic government seemed set fair. The country was once more at peace, and the king, educated in England far away from palace intrigue, had first-hand knowledge of life under parliamentary government. Alfonso XII, furthermore, was a responsible and dedicated man. Nevertheless, the Restoration was, in terms of Spain's well-being, a failure. Alfonso was more Catholic than liberal, and under his rule and that of his second wife, María Cristina of Austria, who became regent when he died of consumption, the Church and the religious orders once more strengthened their hold on Spanish life, re-establishing and extending their privileges and their influence and deliberately stemming the advance of education. Throughout society, enthusiasm for the restored Bourbon monarchy was matched by a renewal of clericalist fervor— frightened by what they had seen of the consequences of liberalism in Spanish politics by "that republic which offered the whole of Spain the spectacle of disorder, with every kind of outrage and injustice," the people were seeking security in reaction.

Perhaps because they sensed this to be the mood of the majority of Spaniards, the country's constitutional leaders in the two decades after the Restoration relieved the voters of the terrible onus of prudent democratic choice. In other words, they rigged the elections, and in so doing did the country, whose welfare some of them had dearly at heart, the worst possible disservice. With the help of powerful local political bosses—*caciques*—the government made sure that in each district its own candidate was returned; given the poverty, ignorance, and illiteracy of the masses, and their dependence for survival in rural districts on rich landlords (who were in most cases the *caciques* themselves), the system was not difficult to work. The result was that instead of slowly educating the people into the duties and responsibilities of par-

This 1901 photograph shows ladies packing cigars in a factory in Seville.

liamentary democracy, Antonio Cánovas del Castillo and Práxedes Sagasta, the leading politicians of these unhealthy years, only led them further into apathy and disillusion with the very concept of stable, representative government. In 1886 the results of the general election which brought Sagasta to power appeared in an official newspaper before polling took place. The granting of universal male suffrage in 1890 was not, consequently, the significant event it should have been.

It must not be thought that this century of inadequacy, corruption, and chaos produced in Spain no courageous, clear-sighted, and enlightened men. On the contrary, Larra was only the first of a growing band of dedicated intellectuals who in their different ways fought for freedom and progress: the radical philosopher Julián Sanz del Río, "the first Spaniard of modern times to go abroad purely for purposes of study," who introduced Spain to German culture; the inspiring and beloved educationalist Francisco Giner de los Ríos with his neat beard, penetrating eyes, and caustic tongue; Joaquín Costa, lawyer and scholar, with his "school and larder" philosophy, which held that citizens well-nourished in mind and body were the first requisite of a healthy nation. From around the middle of the century onward these men and their disciples worked ceaselessly and selflessly for the country they were confident Spain was capable of being. Their overwhelming concern was the education of the young, of those who would eventually be responsible for Spain's future. Their disillusion at the return of the Bourbon monarchy was more than justified, heralding as it did the return of clerical control of education for the following half century. New colleges run by religious orders opened and the handful of private, generally progressive institutions gradually closed. Spanish education soon became as backward and as hidebound by prejudice and ignorance as it had ever been. And the government of Cánovas tried to make sure that all secular teachers conformed; just after Alfonso XII had succeeded to the throne, many of those teachers and professors who refused to do so were sacked and imprisoned—Giner de los Ríos, who occupied the Madrid chair of Natural Law, amongst them. Approved textbooks only were thenceforth to be used and all lectures were to be vetted by the university rectors. The spirit of free inquiry was a notion alien to the meaning of education in Spain.

This repression, however, did not prove entirely sterile, for out of it grew one of the greatest forces for good in Spanish society during the second half of the century and beyond. This was the Institución Libre de Enseñanza, a private day school for boys, founded by Giner to challenge the existing state-and-clergy-controlled system and to show what education in Spain could and should be. Those boys lucky enough to attend received the stimulation of open discussions, expeditions to art galleries, churches, and factories, summer walking tours, and sports. Their schoolmasters became their friends and counselors instead of slave-driving watchdogs.

To us now a day school for around two hundred boys seems a small and insignificant enterprise, yet this institution became famous throughout Europe and is now recognized as having done more to raise the level of Spanish culture than any other institution of its day. At a time when the Church was squeezing what little state education there was out of existence by making sure that funds were not made available, the Free Institute of Education kept Spanish education afloat. And the spirit of the Institution was continued and perpetuated in the Residencia de Estudiantes, a university college in Madrid, and the innovatory Junta para Ampliación de Estudios (Commission for Extension of Studies)—the latter formed by another leading reformer, José Castillejo, to help send students abroad and encourage research.

With the advent of this brave new movement in education, the outlook for the future, in spite of the traditional obstacles, looked very bright indeed, and it is one of the great tragedies of modern Spain that later on in the twentieth century the education movement was ruthlessly crushed by the iron hand of right-wing dictatorship. While it survived, however, it bore glorious fruit, for out of its inspiration there sprang a renaissance of Spanish literature and thought to rival that of Spain's Golden Age. Spanish literature, as Gerald Brenan has said, travels badly, and the political repression of the twentieth century in Spain has not made the journey any easier. Yet modern Spain boasts a literature that stands comparison with that of any other country, characterized above all perhaps by a truly remarkable efflorescence of poetic genius. Out of a long list of names including Miguel de Unamuno, Ramón del Valle Inclán, Pío Baroja, Antonio Machado, Juan Ramón Jiménez, Jorge Guillén, Rafael Alberti, Pedro Salinas, and Federico García Lorca, only the last will probably strike a chord in the memory of most readers. The loss is ours, for apart from creating vibrations which helped revitalize almost every aspect of Spanish culture, these men and others like them have produced work of outstanding literary and human merit. And when political adversity has threatened to stifle their inspiration, they have preferred exile to intellectual sterility.

The rebirth was in a way stimulated by the political and social chaos in which Spain found herself. Spain's great nineteenth-century novelist Benito Pérez Galdós had announced in his historical and contemporary novels the growing concern felt by reformers and intellectuals for Spain's inability to cope with the division and strife within its boundaries or with the modern world outside. The mass of the people, however, lived in the period after the Restoration in a fool's paradise, convinced that with the king once more on his throne all was right with the Spanish world. Their ignorance, their apathy, their complacency, drove the perceptive and informed to despair. The day of reckoning when it came, however, struck the whole of Spain like a thunderbolt, producing reverberations which would ripple through the Spanish consciousness for years to come. The ordinary man in the street stopped short—if only for a brief moment—aghast and incredulous, while the eloquent men of talent were precipitated into a frenzy of self-examination and recrimination and an endless soul-searing search for a solution to the nation's ills.

The year 1898 is a watershed in Spanish history, for in that year Spain lost the last of her colonial possessions. In other words, from 1898 on, Spain no longer had an empire; she stood alone. Throughout the nineteenth century, as she tottered under the tangled burden of political division and civil war, clericalist repression, impatient liberalism, regrettable royal leadership, and *pronunciamientos,* Spain had had somehow to try to cope with an empire champing at the bit to be free of her. Natural allies of one another in a common cause, and with the United States to the north to call on for support, the Central and South American colonies were able to force Spain's hand. After Simón Bolívar led the way in Venezuela in 1811, Peru, Chile, Ecuador, and Mexico achieved independence; the struggles involved Spain in a series of defeats whose implications she was not yet prepared to recognize.

When the end of the century found Spain still hanging on to the remnants of its empire in Central America, Cuba, and the Philippines,

North American involvement was virtually inevitable. The United States had large interests in Cuba. In addition, her natural sympathy with the desire of the New World to break free of the Old was much accentuated by the inhuman campaign of the last Spanish general to command operations in Cuba—Valeriano Weyler. An infamous veteran of the civil troubles in Catalonia, he employed in Cuba combative measures which have become frighteningly familiar—concentration camps and a scorched-earth policy. Spain's decision to recall General Weyler and grant autonomy to Cuba and Puerto Rico came too late for open hostilities to be averted. A little more than two months after the United States battleship *Maine* blew up in Havana harbor in February, 1898, as the result, it was claimed by the United States press, of sabotage, the United States of America declared war. Most of Spain had no conception of the power and resources of their new opponent, and regarded the outbreak of war with the States with feelings ranging only from euphoria to boredom. After two devastating naval disasters in Manila Bay and Santiago de Cuba, the latter on July 3, Spain lost the Philippines, Guam, Cuba, and Puerto Rico and found herself completely denuded of imperial trappings. The response at home was sheer consternation. The last vestiges of greatness had been stripped from Spain with insulting ease by a foreign power, and the blow to Spanish morale was crippling. Perhaps unfairly—for eventual disintegration would seem to be a function of empire—those with the intelligence to care regarded the event as a sign of moral defeat. And those with talent and imagination—Unamuno, Valle Inclán, Baroja, Machado, Azorín, Maeztu, and later Ortega y Gasset among the most prominent—dedicated themselves in their thinking and writing to the quest for Spanish salvation. Their search, which initiated the rebirth of Spanish letters, took them through different fields and along different paths—some seeking the answer in Europe, some in the stuff of Spanish history itself, symbolized for them by the stark grandeur of the Castilian landscape. But their fierce preoccupation with their country made of them a spiritual brotherhood. The spin-off from their activities was varied and prolific—on the one hand an assault upon the exciting cultural and philosophical and political developments of the world outside, on the other hand a stimulating rediscovery of Spain's continuing heritage, which was not only to affect every field of creative activity,

The Spanish-American War was a severe defeat for the already weakened Spain.
Above, a jingoist American cartoon; at right, Spanish prisoners at Guantánamo.

producing figures of such world renown as Pablo Picasso, Joan Miró, and Manuel de Falla, but profoundly influence the directions of Spanish scholarship. But it is the year of lost empire which gives focus and cohesion to this band of men who ushered in a new era for a changed Spain, a Spain forced now to face the future without any comforting delusions of greatness in the world's terms. And appropriately they are known to history, these men who cared and anguished and preached, as the "Generation of '98"—they were the conscience of Spain as it entered our modern era.

As Spain moved out of the nineteenth century and into the twentieth, there was little to inspire Spaniards with confidence in their future. For all the brave efforts of Spanish liberals, the absence of a strong middle class in Spain almost guaranteed the ultimate failure of Spanish liberalism in any meaningful sense. Under the Restoration, trade had expanded, Catalonia had become a flourishing center of light industry, and the Basque country with its mineral ores had witnessed a quite remarkable spurt in heavy industry and banking. But Spain was still predominantly an agrarian community with the mass of its people living at, or below, subsistence level on the land—not by any means a consumer society; and, without an outlet for its products, Spanish industry could not grow beyond a certain point. Spain's social structure, therefore, inhibited both political and economic advance.

The chasm between the rich and poor and the agricultural mismanagement that had bedeviled the economy since the Middle Ages, survived, and would continue to survive, undiminished. A very few examples will serve to recreate the rank flavor of wastage and deprivation. Until the First World War, rich landlords bothered to till only their best lands, and those starving wretches who tried to scratch a living from the neglected soil were beaten for their pains by the police. In the early 1930s, 56,000 acres near Jeréz de los Caballeros were kept uncultivated by their aristocratic owner to serve as a shooting estate. In Andalusia still today thousands of acres of the most fertile land in Spain—a country underendowed with fertile soil—are used for breeding fighting bulls. The efforts made by liberals from the middle of the nineteenth century onward to put Spain's natural resources to more profitable use have, for the most part, failed miserably.

Economic and social conditions at the turn of the century, therefore, had all the makings of trouble. After the failure of liberals to impose liberalism and effective centralist control, Spanish society was possibly more fragmented than it had ever been. To the by now familiar divisions of liberals, intellectuals, conservatives, royalists, and clericals, were added new and less familiar interests and groupings. These were the corrupt and time-serving civil servants concerned only with maintaining the *status quo* which guaranteed them their jobs; the supporters of Catalan independence, resentful of the liberals' reassertion of Castilian centrality; and, most important of all, though not entirely connected with the former, the proletariat, activated by hardship, deprivation, and European example into political consciousness. The proletarian movement itself splintered early on into many subdivisions, chief among them being socialism (centered in Madrid)—a political, normally law-abiding, and centrally organized and oriented movement —and syndicalism or anarchism (centered in Barcelona), which was apolitical, violent, and regional in inspiration. The irreconcilable differences between these representatives of the Spanish left were to influence the fate of Spain profoundly in the years to come.

As all these groups pulled and strained their different ways, the fabric of Spanish society began to wear perilously thin. A nation is, can only be, the product of its history, and for some reason, somewhere along the line, Spaniards had lost sight of the very concept of compromise. The 1890s, which culminated in the great disaster of Cuba in 1898, gave an ominous foretaste of the tragedy that was to result from this intransigence. The decade saw miners' strikes in the Basque country, terrorism and bombings in Barcelona. In 1892 Cánovas admitted to the nation that it was bankrupt, and in the elections that followed, six out of eight seats in Madrid were won by the republican party. The anarchism in Barcelona was eventually countered with measures so repressive that in 1897 Cánovas, head of the Spanish government once more, was assassinated—the first statesman martyred to social strife. Strikes, terrorism, assassinations, repression—all the ingredients for the crisis which was to convulse Spain almost unremittingly for four decades—were now supplied. Few, however, could have foreseen to what lengths the chaos would go, could have dreamed that the forces of right and left, the two Spains, would meet each other halfway only in the tragic expedient of all-out civil war.

CHAPTER VIII

THE CIVIL WAR,
ITS CAUSES
AND ITS AFTERMATH

Spain entered the twentieth century without a king on the throne, but its long and eventful dalliance with monarchy was not by any means yet ended. Alfonso XII had died in 1885 at the early age of twenty-eight, leaving his kingdom with princesses but his wife with child. Six months later María Cristina, to the delight of all save the Carlists, gave birth to a male heir—born a king though not declared of age until he became sixteen in 1902. Throughout her history Spain had had to bear the consequences of an unfair number of infant monarchs—a new reign cannot have the dice loaded against its social and political stability in any surer way. But Alfonso XIII, Spain's last king, proved, on reaching the age when boys are deemed wise enough to rule a nation, not to have profited from his mother's example. He had not inherited his father's ability to play, or at least to seem to play, the constitutional role. Alfonso threw himself into politics and administration more positively than was prudent.

The Spain he inherited needed not a politician on the throne but a gifted diplomat. In the first four years of his reign, Spain had eight prime ministers. In 1906, on the day of his wedding to Queen Victoria's

Picasso captures the mood of his saddened countrymen: with heads bowed by the tragedies of war, they nevertheless remain staunch and dignified.

daughter, Victoria Eugenia, an attempt was even made to assassinate the twenty-year-old king. When some sort of continuity and stability at the top seemed to have been achieved with a conservative administration under Antonio Maura, an explosion of popular resentment eventually forced it out of office after two and a half years.

The events which led to Maura's downfall are significant in that they involved two of the major areas of unrest in the years to come; Morocco and Catalonia. For centuries Spain had kept individual strongholds in Morocco, but in the early 1900s, undeterred by her recent experiences in the Caribbean and the Pacific, she joined France in claiming a shared responsibility for the whole country. In 1909 a column of regular Spanish troops was ambushed and almost wiped out by a mere handful of Berbers—the outcome of sheer incompetence on the part of the Spanish army—and the War Office called on the reserves in Catalonia to replace the dead soldiers. The measure is now accepted to have been almost certainly a deliberately provocative act; Catalonia was already seething with resentment at the government's attitude toward its demands for independence, and with reason. For an English detective brought over by city authorities to investigate the recent extraordinary outburst of terrorism in Barcelona—two thousand bombs thrown, no witnesses, no arrests, and most of the victims Catalan nationalist factory owners—had discovered that the outrages had been committed by gangsters and *agents provocateurs* in the pay of the police.

The government's motive is self-evident: terrorism would justify intervention, that is, repression. It was in fact no accident that the terrorism coincided with a resurgence of the struggle for Catalan autonomy, and after the chief accomplices were tried and convicted, the affair was quickly hushed up.

The result of the draft was catastrophic. For three days Barcelona was given over to mob rule. Twenty-two churches and thirty-four convents were burned, monks were killed, and tombs desecrated, as hatred of the centralist government found expression in an explosion of long-buried resentment against the Church. Workmen drunk with the wine of freedom danced in the streets with the disinterred mummies of nuns. The government showed no mercy in their retaliations. One hundred and seventy-five workmen were shot in the streets, and when calm had been restored the more formal executions took place. Afterward, even the civil governor admitted that to call in the troops against a popular rising organized by no particular left-wing or nationalist group had been a stupid mistake. And the fact that among the executed was the famous anarchist-theoretician Francisco Ferrer, who had not even been implicated in the rising, earned the outraged censure of Europe. It was a gratuitous act of spite against Catalonia and against the left wing, and the country recognized it for what it was. The government fell, and Maura lost the leadership of his party. It would take ten years for the public memory to fade enough to allow him into the political arena again.

In retrospect, the "tragic week" in Barcelona appears as a bitter foretaste of things to come, of the extremes to which the two halves of Spain would go in expressing their fear and hatred of each other. The victimization of the clergy, of course, was not a new phenomenon: throughout the nineteenth century there had been occasional waves of violence against members of the Church. But in the twentieth century the animosity grew. In fact, for all Spain's past, in the first three decades of our era she showed every sign of ceasing to be a predominantly Catholic country. While retaining the outward appearance of orthodoxy by celebrating feast days and festivals, and using the traditional Church offices at birth, marriage, and death, the majority of the people did not go to Mass or confession. By the 1930s in Andalusia only 1 per cent of the male population attended Mass, while of those children educated in convent schools an astonishing total of 90 per cent never went to Mass or confession again after leaving school. As early as 1910 (a year in which the government succeeded in forbidding the foundation of new religious orders) civil marriages were becoming common, indicating that not even social convention was strong enough to stem the rising tide of unbelief.

This picture of Spain may surprise many readers, but it is a picture which explains much about the civil war. Intolerance breeds intolerance, and intolerance of all who did not subscribe to its beliefs was endemic in the Spanish Church. At the end of the century Catholics who ate with Protestants ran the risk of excommunication, and in some places Protestants unfortunate enough to die on Spanish soil are said to have been buried on the shores at low tide. The Freemason was regarded as anti-Christ. Such fanaticism inevitably becomes contagious, and the ferocious hatred that grew up between the Church's followers and opponents found its inevitable outlet in the terrible atrocities of the civil war. In the context of Spain's progress toward secularization during these years, the view that saw the civil war as a crusade dedicated to saving Spain for Christianity becomes comprehensible.

Turmoil, animosity, and simmering revolution—this was Spain as the new century advanced. The geographical fringes strained against the center, clericals and anti-clericals lovingly cultivated their hate, landowners and employers were at daggers drawn with the proletariat and their trade unions, reformers and traditionalists fought over political, educational, and economic issues for the soul of their beleaguered land. Representative government remained discredited, and the army in spite of its unpopularity amongst the common people was fast creating for itself in the minds of other groups the role of the only true repository of Spanish nationalism. Effective reforms were few, and more often than not stillborn; education, for example, was made the responsibility of the State, then allocated such an infinitesimal proportion of the national budget that it virtually remained in the same lamentable condition. And there were other ominous developments: the power of the armed forces was substantially increased by the rule that certain activities against them should be subject to martial law —a guarantee of partiality. In the 1830s Larra had mourned the death of one half of Spain at the hands of the other and it was beginning to be obvious that the needle on the record of Spanish history had stuck.

When the First World War broke out, Spanish sympathies were divided in an entirely predictable way—army, Church, and the right-wingers supporting Germany, while the liberals, the left, and the regional nationalists, in fact the bulk of the population, supported the Allies. The king sat on the fence. Sanity, fortunately, prevailed and Spain stayed out of the conflict, but not unaffected. During these years her industry and trade expanded, largely in response to the needs of the warring nations, and by the end of the war the national debt had been almost redeemed; given social conditions, however, this increased prosperity inevitably led to greater tension between workers and employers. Worse still, prices fell after the war, leading not only to a deep feeling of letdown but also to the specter of unemployment.

The crisis when it came was of the army's making. Its officers being

mainly Andalusians and Castilians, the army's ethos was essentially a centralist one. Resentful of the hate it inspired amongst the working class in Catalonia and the Basque country and impatient with politics in general, it decided to take measures to protect itself. In 1917 the officers in effect created trade unions for themselves—*juntas de defensa*, as they were called. The initial aim of the juntas was the reform of abuses within the army, which squandered funds extravagantly and was hideously underequipped, underpaid (therefore corrupt), and absurdly overmanned: in 1898 there had been a general for every hundred men. It was, in other words, as cumbersome and inefficient a piece of bureaucracy as the Civil Service for which the army professed such scorn.

But although the juntas were at first conceived of as a method of self-reform, and although some of the officers who fathered the idea were supposed to be republicans in the nineteenth-century army tradition, the situation soon changed. By placing its interests before those

Anarchists tried unsuccessfully to assassinate King Alfonso XIII in Madrid on his wedding day in 1906. Alfonso was unhurt but twenty others were killed.

of the country the army made a mockery of constitutional government, and because of its pressures and demands the year 1917 witnessed four successive governments. Anyone who exposed or criticized the army's practices went to prison. Crucial to the army's fast-emerging hegemony was the fact that it had the king's support. Alfonso, for all his ability and undoubted charm, had become by temperament an autocratic king, ignoring the constitution and glorying in the trappings of sovereignty. Like his brother-in-law Kaiser Wilhelm II, he adored the military parades which allowed him to dress in his fine uniforms—he changed his clothes four or five times a day—and to pose and prance dramatically before his subjects, all of whom, except the aristocratic and rich, he referred to as "the *canaille*," or riffraff. The army, he came to regard as his right arm, the extension of his royal will.

The true nature of the army's future role in Spanish politics emerged as the result of a general strike in 1917. Strike leaders had expected it to usher in a new republic. Naively, they counted on army support. But when the troops were called out, they turned their machine guns on the strikers, killed seventy, wounded several hundred, and took two thousand prisoners. The cards were now on the table. The left recognized the army as their enemy, the right hailed it as the savior of the nation. The reality was that from now on the army was the effective power in the land. The king, eager to rule himself through the army, made sure that the political parties, floundering in their accustomed chaos, floundered their way to complete destruction. The day would come when he would have to pay with his throne for this ultimate betrayal of his country, but by then the damage would be done.

Everything pointed to military dictatorship. In Maura's words, "Let those govern who prevent anyone else from doing so." In Catalonia, now pushing for complete autonomy from the country it saw sliding downhill into disaster, industrial strife broke out once more. When negotiations broke down, a hundred thousand workers went out on strike, military law was declared, and in 1921 the prime minister of Spain, Eduardo Dato, was assassinated in Madrid by way of reprisal— he was the tenth prime minister in twenty-five years to be murdered in revenge for police atrocities.

In July of that year, however, the troubled news from Catalonia had been overlaid in people's minds by a military disaster in Morocco.

Impatient with the way affairs in Africa were being handled, the king intervened to direct operations. The outcome was that a twenty-thousand-man column of Spanish soldiers marched across the Riff in a show of force on the very day that the king intended making a speech at the transference of El Cid's remains to Burgos Cathedral. The day chosen for the ceremony was, appropriately, the day of Spain's patron saint, Saint James. The army, however, never arrived. At a place called Annual, it was ambushed by a small force of tribesmen. Ten thousand Spaniards were killed, four thousand taken prisoner, and all the equipment—aircraft included—captured. The Spanish commander killed himself, and two weeks later a key fortress surrendered.

The king, the country knew, was responsible. The commander, acting on the king's orders—"do as I tell you and pay no attention to the minister of war, who is an imbecile"—had led an unprepared and undisciplined force across enemy territory into the arms of death. And such was the impact of the disaster that Spain—except of course the army itself—was now after Alfonso's blood. But on September 23, 1923, seven days before the report of the commission appointed to investigate the disaster, the new captain-general of Catalonia, Miguel Primo de Rivera, saved Alfonso by proclaiming himself dictator.

The new regime was welcomed with enthusiasm by most Spaniards as marking an end to the corruption and inefficiency of the past. It was confidently expected that after Primo de Rivera put the country to rights he would resurrect the suspended constitution. And, indeed, as dictatorships go, his was better than most. Primo was a humane, well-intentioned, garrulous, and gluttonous Andalusian landowner. He worked hard, but also drank hard, and many of his wilder decrees were penned while their author was in no state to think clearly. Cheaply dressed, fussy, and informal, he hardly fills the popular picture of the military dictator. He did, however, have many of the dictator's common drawbacks. He had no experience of government, he despised intellectuals and politicians, and his understanding of economics was extremely shaky. This last weakness proved his downfall. At the beginning of his regime Spain shared in the general European economic boom, but instead of consolidating this position with prudent legislation, Primo frittered Spain's resources away on great public works calculated to bear witness to the country's return to the greatness of its past—harbors, roads, telephones, lavish exhibitions in Seville and Barcelona, and so on. On one occasion when his finance minister managed by means of complicated juggling to make the deficit in the budget disappear, the "quack doctor," as Unamuno scathingly called him, announced that to celebrate the occasion he would redeem all the mattresses that the poor had pawned in the state workshops. A kind, but hopelessly inadequate thought.

And for all his humanity, of course, Primo was a right-wing reactionary. He stamped on Catalan independence, suspended constitutional guarantees, imposed press censorship, and on one occasion closed the University of Madrid for eighteen months. Gradually, in spite of his success in the pacification of Morocco, he lost the support of the people, and even of the army itself. When the world economic crisis of 1929 hit Spain, Primo—now a sick man—was helpless to cope with the complexity of the problem. In the following year he resigned and left the country, for Paris, where he divided his time between Church and brothel, and died within a few months.

Alfonso was left holding the baby, and the people had not forgotten his betrayal of their cause—even lifelong royalists would have nothing to do with him. If a dictator could be got rid of, why not the king? The stopgap solutions aimed at "bringing back the water to the river bed" and saving the king, now virtually bereft of support, came to nothing, and the inevitable had to be faced. But Alfonso himself provided the last straw: in his fight for his throne he made the mistake once again of playing God. At his personal insistence two young rebellious army officers charged with treason were executed in March, 1931. Public opinion was outraged, and in the elections that followed a month later, the people wreaked their revenge. Every provincial capital in Spain but four voted for a republic. Abandoned by the army, the civil guard, and the nobility, the king recognized defeat. He left Madrid and his country on April 14, 1931. Spain had ceased to be a monarchy.

The story of Spain in the next four years is a story of accelerating disaster. The departure of Alfonso, like that of Isabella II in 1868, solved nothing, because, their mutual antagonist removed, the parties and factions once more ceased to agree. Catalonia immediately unbalanced the infant Second Republic by proclaiming her independence, and waves of lawlessness, strikes, and anticlerical violence broke out, so destructive as to necessitate the creation of summary powers of repression and control as regrettable as those of Primo de Rivera's regime. Among the leadership, there was no lack of comprehension of the issues involved, no inability to see what was good, right, and desirable. The difficulty lay in achieving the aims that would so clearly benefit Spain and her people, and the source of the difficulty was the inability of that very people and their leaders to wait, to compromise, to progress slowly.

The leftists and the liberals again made the mistake of thinking that they could educate the people to accept change and reform overnight, forgetting, or choosing to ignore, that there were many who violently disagreed with them. The constitution of 1931 at a stroke disestablished the Church, expelled the Society of Jesus for the second time, allowed divorce by consent, and forbade religious orders to teach. It was a big pill for Spain's believers and traditionalists to swallow, yet the reformers seemed to believe that as if by a wave of a magic wand all would be tolerance, justice, and light. State education in Spain was obviously a highly desirable thing and let it be made clear that in Spain even secular education was at bottom religious, orthodox, and Catholic, taking for granted the Christian and Catholic foundations of Spanish society. The trouble with clericalist teaching was not that it was Catholic but that it was deliberately tendentious and thoroughly bad. The trouble with the republican measures against it was that at the same time that they made it illegal they also made primary education compulsory. Thousands of religious teaching establishments—providing for almost three quarters of the school-age population—were closed and there was nothing to replace them. The result was chaos.

The Republic, in other words, soon proved its own worst enemy, not least by giving the vote to women—traditionally more conservative and church-minded than men. The anticlericalist legislation even caused the first republican prime minister, a conservative Catholic, to resign. The tragedy is that the Republic's policy was an entirely laudable one: to provide the badly needed agricultural reorganization and allow the starving peasants to work the largely neglected territorial empires of the landed aristocrats; to educate the men and women of the future and stamp out illiteracy; to make a success of constitutional government and keep the army and the Church out of it; to

grant the regions autonomy within the nation. But by submitting, as it had to, to the more urgent and extreme demands of Spain's revolutionaries, then trying to incorporate them into the social and economic pattern permitted by antiquated facilities and limited resources, the Republic created tensions which Spain was to prove unable to bear without cracking under the strain. The rich were alienated in order to succor the poor, the poor were alienated because they wanted more than the government was immediately able to give. The new Spain that the republicans wished to build was too new for one half of the country, not new enough for the other. The two halves were fast becoming irreconcilable.

Disappointment and frustration had their effect. In the November elections of 1933 the republicans were crushingly defeated by the forces of the right who were spurred into antagonism by the government's concessions to revolution and its incapacity to cope with the consequences, and by those of the left, to whom so much had been promised and so little given. There followed two years of center-right government, called by Spanish historians the *"bienio negro"*—the black biennium: black because many of the reforms of the previous two years were repealed and the machinery for impending reform ground to a halt. Discontent spread like wildfire. Groupings splintered and multiplied to center, left, and right in kaleidoscopic confusion as the Republic tried to grope its way toward a solution.

In October, 1934, a cabinet reshuffle further toward the right precipitated a general strike. Riots and church-burnings followed. Catalonia again declared independence, and the army—now clearly aligned with the right—was called in to quell the revolt. In Asturias a more significant rebellion—almost a small civil war—broke out which, to the ferocious resentment of the people, was crushed with unforgivable barbarity by the Spanish Foreign Legion and Moroccan troops. The result was slaughter. More than three thousand were killed and seven thousand wounded (both the dead and the wounded were mostly miners), and while the battle raged no prisoners were taken. The tortures and executions followed. The center of Oviedo, including the university, was almost destroyed and the cathedral badly damaged. The symbolic significance of the dispatch of Moroccan troops to fight Asturian miners was not lost on a nation which had never forgotten

Barcelona, a center of artistic and industrial progressivism, was patron to Antonio Gaudi; his Church of the Sagrada Familia was begun in 1883.

its emergence from that same province of Asturias in defiance of its Islamic conquerors. And not lost on us now is the fact that the man who dispatched the Moroccans was a general with a record of service in North Africa called Francisco Franco.

By now the Republic seemed to be facing insurmountable obstacles. By the end of 1935 there had been twenty-eight governments in five years. An effort to secure the elections of February, 1936, for the left resulted in the formation of a Popular Front, consisting of republicans, socialists, syndicalists, anarchists, and communists. The front gained a sweeping victory in the Cortes, though it must be mentioned, in view of events to come, that in terms of votes the results were very close.

The new government itself was not a left-wing coalition—the parties had agreed to present a common front only in order to secure the elections and indeed refused to sit in a joint cabinet. The extreme left agitated and the extreme right was ruthless in manufacturing incidents to provoke outbreaks of violence. In the summer months of 1936 the right as a whole was panicked by the swing of popular support away from Manuel Azaña, the creator of the "bourgeois republic," toward the socialist Largo Caballero, already dubbed by *Pravda* the Spanish Lenin. And the socialists themselves were confident that their paradise was in sight. Their ingrained antagonism toward the Republic, however, was to ensure that even republicanism, let alone socialism, was something Spain would not be allowed to enjoy for very much longer.

The army and the Falange—the Spanish fascist movement founded by Primo de Rivera's son José Antonio—were laying their plans. Both the Falange and communism gathered momentum through these months as if in preparation for the international struggle between fascism and communism that was to take place on Spanish soil. But while communism was only effective in dissipating support for the left by undermining working-class solidarity, the Falange was busy consolidating support for the right. The Falange was also more ruthless in the realization of its aims. Its tactics were terrorism, murder, and violence and in Madrid cars of hired assassins armed with machine guns toured the streets shooting down known opponents. For all their brutal methods the Falangists found disparate but willing allies in the Church, the Carlists, and monarchists, as well as in the army itself.

While the left squabbled and the right plotted, they dragged the

country down into a chaos from which there seemed no escape—
strikes, hunger, unemployment, accelerating economic depression,
shooting matches between socialists and the Falange in Madrid, church-
burnings, and endless factional collision. Under the leadership of José
Calvo Sotelo the right itched for total rebellion. The procession of ten
thousand workmen through Madrid on May 1 shouting, "We want a
Workers' Government. Long live the Red Army," only confirmed their
sense of urgency.

On July 13 Calvo Sotelo was assassinated by socialist activists in
reprisal for the murder of one of their fellows by the Falange. The date
of the projected rising was brought forward, and on July 16 the Spanish
army in Morocco rose and occupied Ceuta and Melilla. In the afternoon
of the following day almost every garrison in Spain rose against the
government. They expected to reclaim Spain for Catholicism, Con-
servatism, and Tradition, that is, for the Past. And they expected to do
so in the space of a few days. It took them three tragic years.

The Spanish civil war has left a scar on the soul of Spain that will
take a long time to eradicate completely. It left a million Spaniards
dead and much of the country in ruins. It divided families and evinced
extremes of savagery and heroism. It drew upon Spain the anxious eye
of a world itself soon to be engulfed in a war with almost identical
issues at stake. For, viewed in bold relief, the Spanish civil war was a
microcosmic prologue to the battle between fascism and democracy
that was the Second World War. And indeed, while France and England remained officially neutral as they waited for the outcome with
bated breath, the other powers striving to dominate the European
scene—Germany, Italy, and Russia—used Spain as a training ground
for the apocalyptic struggle to come. Russia poured in aid for the left,
hoping thus to help bring about a communist Spain. Italy and Germany
poured in aid for the right hoping to secure the Peninsula and its won-
derful strategic position for fascism. In the middle the Spanish people
fought, starved, and died for their beliefs, or for those that were forced
upon them. And for all their spirit, for all their courage, it was foreign
help that decided the outcome. That supplied by Germany and Italy
was more powerful, and the nationalists accordingly won the war.

The international perspective, however, though important, over-
looks the enormous complexity of the war from the Spanish point of

In a series of tormented images, Picasso's painting inspired by the bombing of Guernica in 1937 expresses the pointless violence of war.

view. There are many aspects of it which are not adequately understood by the general public abroad. To begin with, the republicans, reds, or loyalists, as they were variously called, represented the legitimate government of Spain and continued to do so until the end of the war. The nationalists, as right-wing revolutionaries, were the rebels. On the other hand, the conflict was far from being a straightforward struggle between the people and the army. The country was split down the middle in an alignment of interests which was not always a wholehearted one but which circumstances made necessary. The groupings on the right formed bedfellows as uneasy as those on the left, but to anyone on the right a right-wing antagonist was infinitely preferable to a left-wing one and vice versa. Thus, the Falange—antimonarchist, antiregionalist, and basically anticlericalist—sided with the Carlists, who were dedicated to a Catholic monarchy and regional autonomy, while they in turn nonetheless sided with the essentially centralist army. The Church and the aristocracy naturally supported the right against the left, which was particularly hostile to their interests. The parties of the Popular Front, equally naturally, arranged themselves in opposition. But in the middle were conflicts of interests which had to be painfully decided one way or the other, according to priorities. Thus the agricultural provinces, which could ultimately only lose if a right-wing government ousted the Republic, threw their lot in with the nationalists on grounds of religion. While the Basque country was bitterly divided into two, one half putting their Catholicism before their desire for independence and joining the right, the other half remaining staunch to the ideal of Basque independence and joining the left. The fact that the issue of regionalism made Catalonia, Valencia, and half the Basques republicans but did not prevent the Carlists from becoming nationalists, reveals the enormous complexity of the war and of Spanish politics as a whole.

Until the impact of German and Italian artillery and aircraft started to make itself felt, the outcome of the war was in doubt. In fact at times it seemed as if the republicans might prevail. For although the nationalists had at their disposal most of the armed forces in the country, including the Civil Guard and the Foreign Legion, they were not adequately trained or equipped for war. And the republicans, while they had to drill an army almost from scratch, had the northern and eastern industrial complex, the enthusiastic support of the industrial masses, and legitimacy on their side. In Madrid and Barcelona, the main loyalist strongholds of the war, these rose as one against the insurgents and swept them into the dust. The workers in fact soon took the defense of the country into their own hands, setting up Workers' Committees to organize and arm a militia. This, of course, was in its own way an act of rebellion, and the great tragedy of the left was that the government continued to be the victim of the vicissitudes of left-wing political opinion. The Workers' Committees had brushed aside the liberal republicans and they in turn gave way to a Popular Front government under Largo Caballero. In the second year of the war the anarcho-syndicalists created a war within the war by attempting to wrest power from the republican government. They even set up a rival administration in their headquarters, Barcelona; so that when the government after moving from Madrid to Valencia was forced to retreat north to Barcelona itself, there were two governments in the one city. The right, on the other hand, possessing no legal position of authority as yet to squabble over, was persuaded to forget its differences in the cause of a common goal—victory. The persuader was a figure the left lacked—a charismatic leader.

In October, 1936, General Franco emerged from the trio of nationalist commanders—Franco himself, Emilio Mola, and Gonzalo Queipo de Llano—as the right's supreme warlord and was proclaimed Generalissimo, Head of State. Hitler's judgment on this was: "The real tragedy for Spain was the death of Mola [in an air crash]; there was the real brain, the real leader. . . . Franco came to the top like Pontius Pilate in the Creed." But Hitler by this time was soured by Franco's obstinacy in keeping Spain out of the Second World War, and in spite of the fact that Franco's rise to power was largely due to the strength of his Moroccan army, he did in fact prove to be exactly what the nationalists needed. Apart from being a highly competent general—he had after all been one since the age of thirty-two—he owed allegiance to no obvious political party. He was therefore able to create for the nationalist cause an image that transcended politics, that stood for a united, orderly, and Catholic Spain faithful to the great legacy of the past. His strength lay in his own complete belief in this historic ideal, and the iron will and self-control which enabled him to impose it upon potentially recalcitrant factions like the Carlists and the Falange, neither of whom, at bottom, he had much time for. And at the instigation of his brother-in-law, the lawyer Ramón Serrano Suñer, he set about making the nationalist state a viable alternative to the Republic by evolving a juridical policy on this basis, and transforming "an insurrection into a political enterprise."

While republicans and nationalists fought over the stricken body of Spain, the sympathies of the democratic West were overwhelmingly on the side of the left. For a complex of reasons that included fear of a general war and fear of communism, the governments stood by and watched republican Spain go under. But many individuals reacted to the crisis with selfless enterprise and courage. Centers for refugee children were established, financial aid was organized, and fishing boats helped in the relief of beleaguered coastal towns. The hearts of the young, particularly of young intellectuals, writers, and artists, were with the Republic. And many of them—Ernest Hemingway and George Orwell amongst the most famous—joined the International Brigade (which eventually boasted two American battalions and one British as well as those of other nations) and fought on Spanish soil for what they believed was right. The disillusion experienced by many of them on discovering that they had joined what had become not so much a fight for democracy as an attempt at a communist take-over was a bitter pill to swallow. But fascism was the deadlier enemy, and those who fought and survived could never reconcile themselves to the nationalist victory. Thousands who were young then and who did not actually throw themselves physically into the struggle have not been able to bring themselves to set foot in Spain since. For them—and they come from all parties, creeds, and walks of life—the Spanish civil war and its outcome was a betrayal of all they held dear. It was the "last great enterprise."

It was the Spaniards themselves, however, who had to live through the war and its aftermath. Whichever side they were on, there were foreign airplanes, tanks, and artillery, there were fifth columnists creating tension and suspicion, and above all there was the fear of conquest. For many loyalty was an accident of geography: they happened to live in a committed region or they were engulfed by the swing of battle. Extremadura and much of Andalusia, for example, which had voted for the Popular Front, soon became nationalist owing to the fortunes of war. Life under these circumstances was very difficult unless one became a convinced supporter of the victorious side. And life was in any case difficult enough. Both sides tried to organize their resources and introduce legislation so that existence of a sort could continue, but the level of deprivation, particularly in rural areas, was appalling. The republican zone, in particular, suffered, since the nationalist territory included the main food-producing zones, and strict rationing had to be introduced. The nationalists for their part, always better organized, managed to develop a more or less viable economy. This naturally did little to help the republican cause.

Worst of all was the atmosphere of hatred and dread that was the outcome of the inevitable atrocities. As the separate zones crystallized and distinct front lines of battle emerged, the horror of the situation abated somewhat and in many areas a semblance of normal living was achieved. But as in any civil war the cumulative effect of violence was horrific. Even before the war, as we saw, the extreme right and left had not balked at gratuitous violence. Now with all restraints, particularly on the nationalist side, removed, the long years of buried resentment welled to the surface and exploded into viciousness. In the Red Terror of the first two months, mobs reacted to the news of nationalist air raids or atrocities with mass executions of fascist suspects taken from prisons. Others were taken from their houses at night and carried away in lorries to their deaths. The republicans were appalled. It was news of the massacre at republican Badajoz, however, that drove them to act. Moroccan troops, and legionaires singing their regimental hymn which proclaimed death to be their bride, had stormed the city and fought their way in. Hand-to-hand fighting throughout the day had turned the city into a blood bath and even the capture of the city failed to stop the killing. Two militiamen were slaughtered on the steps of the high altar of the cathedral, and hundreds more who had been disarmed were shot down in the bull ring. German officers later testified to seeing many castrated corpses, although General Franco had forbidden his troops to treat the bodies of their victims in the traditional Moroccan way. To prevent mass murder of nationalist political prisoners in retaliation for this brutal episode, the government acted quickly and set up a Revolutionary Tribunal for the punishment of war crimes. After this, unauthorized executions became very rare in the republican zone.

In the nationalist zone suspected sympathizers or "unacceptable persons" fared less well. Thousands and thousands of people were executed as old scores were paid off, as the old parties of the right revenged themselves for the years of humiliation under the Republic. Queipo de Llano's propaganda chief could eventually no longer stand the horror of his job and fled abroad. The murder was totally indiscriminatory. On the night of August 18, 1936, either the Civil Guard or the Falange entered the house of one of the fascist leaders in Granada—who happened to be away—and carried off into the distant countryside a friend of the family. There, in a ravine, he was made to dig his own grave and then he was shot. The man was Federico García Lorca, the most gifted poet and dramatist of his generation, perhaps of modern Spain, who had once prophetically described the Civil Guard as having hearts as well as hats of patent leather. To this day it is not known why Lorca—an artist with little interest in politics though admittedly with many socialist friends—was murdered. Perhaps it was because he happened to be the brother-in-law of the socialist mayor of Granada, who had been dragged through the streets to his execution. Or perhaps it was just because he was an artist—a less conventional and more colorful figure than the normal run of Spaniards and therefore offensive to those for whom nonconformity was a sure sign of left-wing subversion. Thousands of people were put to death for similar reasons, for being what they were and not for any political affiliations—Freemasons for being Freemasons, Protestants for being Protestants, and, on the other side at the beginning, the rich and the middle class for being rich or middle class. After the war Lorca became for the world the supreme sacrificial symbol of the wasteful brutality of these three years. And so embarrassed was Franco's Spain by the world's outrage at this senseless destruction of genius, that after ten years of sullen silence the right-wing groups, pressured at last into speaking, scrambled to exonerate themselves from blame, each condemning the other for the crime. But Lorca still lies buried in an unidentified grave.

The pointless killings, the inhuman tortures, rapes, and victimization of the early period were accompanied, of course, and overtaken by the no less brutal ebb and flow of war. It was a war which like most had its epic moments, and on both sides. The nationalist defenders of Gijón

in Asturias rather than surrender radioed the following message to a nationalist warship lying off the town: "Defense is impossible. The barracks are burning and the enemy are starting to enter. Fire on us!" The request was obeyed. The ancient fortress city of Toledo with its staunchly Catholic inhabitants, held out against the republican besiegers for months. It's heroic commander, General José Moscardó, refused to exchange the arsenal for his captured son; he was rewarded for this personal sacrifice by the arrival at last, after the inhabitants of the alcazar had been reduced to eating rats, of relief forces. The record of this event reveals just how ferocious were the loyalties at stake. To his father over the phone the boy said, "they say they will shoot me if the alcazar does not surrender." "If it be true," replied his father, "commend your soul to God, shout Viva España, and die like a hero. Goodbye my son, a last kiss." "Goodbye father," came the reply, "a very big kiss." "The alcazar will never surrender," said General Moscardó to his son's captors before he hung up. And it did not. Nor was the son shot on that occasion. But he was shot a month later in reprisal for an air raid. The nationalists later did not omit to make the attackers

Nationalist troops, equipped for gas warfare, stand for review in 1938.

pay for this. When they captured the town, now apart from the alcazar occupied by the republicans, the main street ran with blood down the hill to the city gates.

On the republican side two events above all stand out from the maelstrom of battle and death. One is the three-year-long defense of the capital, Madrid, during which repeated assaults from without were repelled and subversion within was fought in running street battles. Children helped build barricades, women formed their own battalion, and Spain's most famous communist, the Asturian miner's wife Dolores Ibarruri, nicknamed La Pasionaria (the Passionflower), toured the streets with a loudspeaker urging housewives to prepare boiling oil with which to protect their homes. The other was the terrible destruction of the small Basque town of Guernica, the historical home of Basque liberties, which was nineteen miles distant from the front. On the afternoon of April 26, 1937, German bombers, for no conceivably important strategic reason, dropped waves of incendiary bombs and high explosives upon the town every twenty minutes for three and a quarter hours. The townsfolk (there were only seven thousand in all) who ran from the rain of fire were machine-gunned from the air. Apart from the Basque parliament house and the oak tree where since time immemorial Spanish monarchs had sworn their willingness to observe Basque rights, the little town was flattened. (Not until 1946 did

The grim face of civil war: injured refugees hurrying to the French border; a lone soldier fighting beside a fallen comrade amid the ruins of a farmhouse

Göring admit that the Germans had used Guernica as a testing ground for their aerial strategies.) Pablo Picasso, then honorary director of the Prado museum, immediately began his most famous work, the mural "Guernica"—symbol for him of the horror of all war, and the symbol for the world of the tragedy that was the Spanish civil war. For a long time after they had been evacuated to England, the Basque children when given crayon and paper to draw on could draw nothing but falling bombs.

On January 26, 1939, Barcelona fell to the nationalist forces. In Madrid the war came to an end with a six-day civil war between the communists and the Defense Committee set up in opposition to them by an army commander, Colonel Casado, who hoped to negotiate a truce with Franco; to the last the left was the victim of its own internal squabbles. The struggle effectively put an end to republican resistance. On March 28, Madrid and the Republic surrendered. At General Franco's insistence the surrender was unconditional. The Spanish civil war was over.

About fifty miles to the northwest of Madrid, in the middle of the starkly splendid Castilian countryside, there is a large, green, and richly treed park. It is called the Valley of the Fallen, dedicated by Franco to the victims of the civil war, all the victims. If, however, one goes inside the great basilica sunk into the mountain's side with its gigantic cross towering above, and reads the inscriptions and the carved prayers of thanksgiving, one does not for long remain in any doubt about whom the monument in fact commemorates. There is buried the hero of nationalist Spain, José Antonio Primo de Rivera, executed by the left in 1939, who had he lived would have been a sure rival for supreme power. And there, in accordance with his wishes, Franco's body will be taken when he dies. Popular rumor has it that this memorial to the dead heroes of Spain was in fact built by the "wrong" half of those that survived, by concentration camp laborers paying for their protracted resistance with the toil and tears of humiliation and defeat. Not until 1945, six and a half years after the war ended, was a political amnesty proclaimed.

There still remain many of the left who dare not return to Spain. Immediately after the war they faced the choice of imprisonment (or worse) or exile, and in this way the country lost to the world, particularly to the two Americas, the intellectual and artistic flower of a whole generation. Those they left behind, those of the right and those, after they had paid the price of their affiliation, of the no longer apparent left, settled down to life in a dictatorship, with all that that entailed: restriction, repression, censorship, enforced conformity, whispers, and fear. In the new constitution that was written, the anticlerical legislation of the Republic was repealed, and the clergy and aristocracy contentedly settled back again into their positions of unassailable privilege, the Church enjoying a greater position of authority than it had done since the seventeenth century. The Jesuits were reinstated with even greater rights than before, religious education was brought back, and the divorce law was repealed.

Franco won the war only to find himself ostracized as a result by the world. His pact with Nazi Germany did nothing to enhance nationalist Spain in the eyes of the Allies, and the governments who had stood by and watched government by consent engulfed by insurrection now condemned the new regime for its authoritarianism. In December, 1946, Spain was formally ostracized by the United Nations. Governments, however, have short memories when it suits them. In 1953 the United States decided it could swallow its principles and grant Spain economic aid in return for the defense bases it wished to establish on Spanish soil. American acceptance was the foot in the door, and two years later Spain gained admittance to the United Nations. No one can begrudge Spain the benefits of that American aid. In the years immediately after the terrible destruction of the war, as she struggled to get back on her feet, she suffered grinding poverty and hardship. But neither can it be denied that American money, by putting Spain on the road toward economic recovery, helped consolidate Franco's regime. On September 26, 1953, Spain signed the treaty. That evening Franco remarked to his friends: "At long last I have won the Spanish war."

There is no doubt that over the last fifteen or so years Spain has achieved a degree of prosperity that she has never before known. Industry, agriculture, and education have received a share of the national budget. Factories have sprung up, harvesting combines have appeared on the land, and bold reforestation schemes have gotten underway. But to keep this progress in perspective we must bear in mind that the whole of Europe has experienced a phenomenal leap in the standard of living and that Spain could hardly fail to benefit from the general upward trend. In view of this fact, Spain's progress has been very modest. Thousands of Spaniards still have to keep two jobs in order to make a living wage and, although secondary education is compulsory and many state schools have been built, thousands of Spanish children cannot go to school because they have to contribute to the financial upkeep of the family. In rural areas poverty is very apparent. The educational system and the level of instruction in schools and universities leaves a great deal to be desired: the lack of libraries and other facilities, particularly for scientific research, is crippling. And if opportunity is the true measure of the successful, modern state, then Spain has still a great deal of leeway to make up—the child born in one of Spain's out-of-the-way crumbling hamlets has virtually no chance of ever escaping from his rural prison.

Politically, American aid and entry into the United Nations did not bring any repeal of the restrictions on human liberty. Political parties and propaganda are forbidden and the press is controlled. The trade unions, first state- and later craft-controlled, have no official political affiliation, and the Cortes, reinstated by Franco, although representative of all classes and occupations in Spain, has no political basis. In 1966 Spanish heads of families and their wives were given the right to vote a hundred members—two per province—into the Cortes, but again not on the basis of political views. They could choose which individual they preferred, but only from a preselected pool of candidates —all of whom could be guaranteed to be of impeccable loyalty to Franco. In late years a few steps toward greater freedom have been taken in response to pressure from enlightened administrators, from the industrial workers, and from a more progressive papacy. But the agitation for further liberties which was the outcome of this has on occasion provoked Franco into hasty backpedaling. In 1968 a state of exception was proclaimed which after the gradual loosening up of the previous few years subjected Spain and Spaniards once more to rigid state control. The enormous influx of tourists, enthusiastically encouraged by the Spanish government, has of course had its effect in fostering knowledge and acceptance of the world and its ways; and to the tourist, Spain is a lively, picturesque, bustling, and flourishing place to visit. And so indeed it is. So much so that it is difficult at times to remember that behind the facade of the beautiful cities with their elegant shops, packed restaurants, fine public buildings, and splendid country-side, now virtually free of Civil Guards, the ever-ready truncheons and the iron hand that gives them their authority, and against which there is no sure legal appeal, still lurk.

The source of the problem is not so much Franco and his regime as the fact that the two Spains still exist and that Franco has tried to rule in full cognizance of this. In the circumstances he has managed very respectably. Thirty-one years of peace and stability and even modest progress is not a fact which Spain in the light of its history can despise. Neither is Franco's agility in having kept Hitler and Germany at bay and Spain out of the Second World War: Hitler's bitterness went so far as to wish that Falangists and Reds might join together "to rid themselves of the clerico-monarchical muck" which had floated to the top of postwar Spain. Franco himself has never had any doubt of the nature of his role. The 1958 constitution begins: "I, Francisco Franco Bahamonde, Caudillo of Spain, Mindful of my responsibility before God and before History and in the presence of the Cortes of the Kingdom, promulgate the following Principles of the National Movement, as a communion of Spaniards dedicated to the ideals that gave birth to the Crusade."

And in his own lights he has fulfilled it. In many ways an enigmatic figure, this ascetic, controlled man has dedicated himself to his country, and no breath of personal scandal of any sort has ever tainted the image he has sought to project. Seeing himself as the incarnation and symbol of historic Spain, he has behaved accordingly, personally and politically, even when this meant a clash with Rome as the result of his insistence on exercising the traditional privilege of the Spanish monarchs. In order to do so he has had to evolve his own brand of compromise government. For the divisions of the right did not disappear with the war. Franco has had to use all his military authority and all his political astuteness to maintain an equilibrium between Falange, Church, monarchists, and army. All his policies have had somehow to circumvent, or else allow for, the vested interests of one or more of these groups. Moreover, all movement has been circumscribed by fear of the dead but by no means buried left. The thought that concessions, however desirable, might prove the thin end of the wedge must have

been one of the greatest barriers to speedier progress. The need to mollify the right and maintain himself in power, and to present to the world a reasonably acceptable image without encouraging the left, has forced Franco to be an expert juggler.

Not that on occasion he has not hesitated to displease a section of the right. Since 1947 when a referendum on the subject was held, Franco, to the fury of the antimonarchist Falange, has been committed to restoring the monarchy. In fact after that date Spain was officially a monarchy without a king, as the word "kingdom" in the piece quoted above from the constitution indicates. What sort of monarchy Franco envisages is a different matter—it is certainly not a constitutional one

Franco's influence can be seen as retrogressive, even villainous, by some, while for others he is the shining symbol of a restored and reunited Spain.

in a free democracy. And unwilling to take the risk, Franco has proved reluctant to relinquish power in his lifetime. Alfonso XIII's son, Juan, has waited in the wings for years in Portugal, vainly expecting to be called. In order to postpone the day of decision, Franco has chosen to bestow his favor instead upon Juan's son, Juan Carlos. At Franco's instigation Prince Juan Carlos was given the training appropriate to the heir of the throne, and in 1969 Franco proclaimed him future king and chief of state, Spanish law providing for the naming of a prime minister to head the government sometime in the indefinite future. In the summer of 1971, with Franco seventy-eight years old, an official state bulletin decreed that the prince should stand in for Franco as chief of state whenever the Caudillo is absent or ill. Obviously, the day when Spain once more becomes a monarchy is now deemed to be within sight.

What sort of a monarch Juan Carlos will be, or what sort of monarch he will be allowed to be, only the future will show. And for Spain the future is in all ways uncertain. It may well be true that 60 per cent of the population would probably welcome an end to the authoritarian regime, but it is even more certain that most do not want it at the cost of renewed civil strife. Even Franco's regime, which has not since the early years been (as dictatorships go) an intolerable one, has not been proof against signs, at least, of the seething political activity below the apparently calm surface of Spanish life. There have been Falange demonstrations, miners' strikes, and student riots. University lectures have been suspended and professors dismissed. Progressive priests have supported industrial agitation, and not long ago there was a fierce upsurge of Basque independence. Order has been restored by means of brute force, people have been imprisoned, tortured, and have died. Cabinets have been reshuffled in an attempt to produce the combination that would solve the conflict without betraying the principles of the national movement so dear to Franco's heart. In recent years the ministers and administrators of the old military guard with their eyes on the past have been gradually replaced with young, efficient, and modern-minded technocrats, hand-picked, for all that, for their apparent committal to the basic principles of the Franco regime. Many of them are members of the *Opus Dei,* the enormously powerful lay religious order founded in 1928 by José María Escrivá Balaguer in an attempt to make of religion a meaningful and influential thing in the modern world.

A semisecret society regarded with some suspicion by the Church, its members pledge their lives and their work to God. The order has in the last few years gained a remarkable ascendancy in governmental and professional circles in Spain, an ascendancy shaken but not toppled in 1969 by the Matesa affair. When this scandal concerning misappropriation of tax credits by a large textile firm came to light, a number of government officers, including some associated with the Opus Dei, were implicated. It so shocked the nation that Franco, after initially trying to suppress the furor, ordered a full-scale inquiry, and drastically reshuffled the cabinet. Everything points to the Opus Dei's being one of the most influential factors in the Spain of the future.

The Spain of the present, meanwhile, waits. It is aware of what needs to be done and is eager to do it. The 1969 White Book on education, which—encouragingly—took a frank and honest look for the first time since the war at the state of education at all levels in Spain, was sold out within ten days when it appeared. But if and how the reformation will come about is an imponderable. So too is the question of who will replace Franco as head of the government when he dies. Franco himself is as adamant as always that democracy is not the answer for Spain: "Let Spaniards remember that each nation is a prey to its particular furies, and that they are different in each case. Spain's furies are the anarchical spirit, negative criticism, lack of solidarity between men, mutual enmity. Any political system which nurtures in its bosom the fostering of these defects, the setting loose of these familiar Spanish furies, will sooner or later—much more probably sooner than later—wreak havoc on all material progress and all improvements of our citizens' lives." These are the sentiments usually favored by dictators who seek to justify themselves, but Spanish history so far has proved Franco right. Whether his judgment is as accurate a forecast of the future, only time and Spain will decide. When Joaquín Costa at the turn of the century said to Giner de los Ríos: "Giner, we want a man," Giner answered: "Joaquín, what we want is a people." Spain needs both if the future is to be in any way bright. One hopes that like other nations who have won through division to stability, she will find them.

CHRONOLOGY

1478	Isabella establishes the Inquisition to crush heresy
1479	Aragon and Castile are united under the joint rule of Ferdinand and Isabella, the "Catholic Monarchs"
1492	The fall of Granada; the expulsion of Jews from Castile; the discovery of America by Columbus
1516–1556	Reign of Charles I (*first of the Hapsburg rulers*); age of the conquistadors and exploitation of New World wealth
1540	Ignatius of Loyola founds the Jesuits in Rome
1556–1598	Reign of Philip II; era of Spanish military supremacy; the capital is established at Madrid; the Escorial is built
1567	The Netherlands begins wars of independence from Spain
1571	Don John of Austria's naval victory over the Turks at Lepanto
1588	Defeat of the Invincible Armada by England
1605	Publication of first part of Cervantes' *Don Quijote*
1609	Spain expels the *Moriscos,* Christianized Moslems
1621–1665	Reign of Philip IV; Spain enters period of decadence
1700–1746	Reign of Philip V (*first of the Bourbon rulers*)
1701–1715	War of the Spanish Succession
1759–1788	Reign of Charles III, Spain's most enlightened despot
1793	The French Republic declares war on Spain
1805	Spain enters the War of the Third Coalition against England; Nelson destroys Spain's fleet at Trafalgar
1807	French armies invade Spain; Charles IV abdicates; Joseph Bonaparte (Napoleon's brother) takes the throne
1808–1814	England launches the Peninsular War (the Spanish War of Independence) to help rid Spain of French occupiers
1812	Liberals create the first national constitution
1814–1833	Restoration of Ferdinand VII; persecution of liberals; South American colonies fight for independence
1833–1868	Reign of Isabella II; Carlist wars break out
1873–1874	The First Spanish Republic is proclaimed
1875–1885	Restoration of monarchy under Alfonso XII
1898	The Spanish-American War
1902–1931	Reign of Alfonso XIII, Spain's last monarch
1914	Spain declares neutrality in World War I
1931	The Second Republic is established
1933	Founding of the Falange, the Spanish fascist party
1936	The Popular Front, a leftist coalition, wins general elections
1936–1939	The Spanish civil war; rightist insurgents, or nationalists, fight leftist republicans, or loyalists; General Franco of the rightists wins the final victory
1939–1945	Spain remains neutral in World War II
1955	Spain is admitted to the United Nations
1969	Franco proclaims Alfonso XIII's grandson, Prince Juan Carlos, Spain's future king and head of state

CREDITS AND INDEX

Page numbers in **boldface type** refer to illustrations.
Page references to map entries are in *italic type*.